WHAT
LOSS
CAN
TEACH
US

WHAT LOSS CAN TEACH US

A Sacred Pathway
to Growth and Healing

Beth Taulman Miller

UPPER
ROOM BOOKS®
NASHVILLE

Cover design: Amanda Hudson, Faceout Studio
Cover imagery: Stocksy
Interior design and typesetting: PerfecType | Nashville, TN

Library of Congress Cataloging-in-Publication Data
Names: Miller, Beth Taulman, 1966- author.
Title: What loss can teach us : a sacred pathway to growth and healing /
  Beth Taulman Miller.
Description: Nashville, TN : Upper Room Books, 2021. | Includes
  bibliographical references.
Identifiers: LCCN 2020034267 (print) | LCCN 2020034268 (ebook) | ISBN
  9780835819619 (paperback) | ISBN 9780835819626 (mobi) | ISBN
  9780835819633 (epub)
Subjects: LCSH: Loss (Psychology)--Religious aspects--Christianity. |
  Suffering--Religious aspects--Christianity. | Spiritual exercises.
Classification: LCC BV4905.3 .M54 2021 (print) | LCC BV4905.3 (ebook) |
  DDC 248.8/6--dc23
LC record available at https://lccn.loc.gov/2020034267
LC ebook record available at https://lccn.loc.gov/2020034268

To Sheryl, for helping me welcome what loss could teach me and doing so with such tender strength. I am forever grateful.

And in memory of my dad, Jim Taulman. One of the ways I'm learning to be in the world without you is to stay awake to the things your dying has taught me.

She could never go back and make some of the details pretty. All she could do was move forward and make the whole beautiful.

—Terri St. Cloud

So let us pick up the stones over which we stumble, friends, and build altars.

—Pádraig Ó Tuama

CONTENTS

CONTENTS

ACKNOWLEDGMENTS

Michael, Joanna, and the team at The Upper Room, I am so grateful for your belief in this book and for bringing it to fruition. Michael, thank you for your steady kindness and generous support in the face of my questions/vulnerabilities/freak-outs.

Becky, thanks for getting me started that day at Starbucks. Your encouragement as a friend and a writer was significant and gave me the traction I needed.

Ross West and Carolyn Gregory, through your helpful editing of my proposal, I felt the support by proxy from my Dad. He would have loved that you were a part of this with me. Thank you.

To those of you who read this whole thing or pieces of it in its multiple drafts, I am so incredibly grateful for the time you invested in giving me your feedback. It's such a better book because of your input.

To the Marriage Matters Community, thank you for being such a safe place to land. Being surrounded by you in those early days was one of the many ways God loved me well. I'm grateful for the support and wisdom you showed us as we walked a road that many of you had already traveled.

Lisa, thank you for good conversation around so many things—but specifically, what it means to live into a Larger Story. I look forward to many more good conversations (as well as the wine and cheese plates that usually accompany them).

Pam, Mary Beth and Susan, thank you for speaking into my life and pointing the way toward health.

Mel, Eva, and Sue, thank you for sharing the wisdom you've gleaned over the years as you've walked with others in spiritual direction, and specifically for sharing with me meaningful practices for navigating the dark night of the soul.

Deb, those days in December of 2005 with you and Mark were life changing for us. You spoke words of hope that were clearly grounded in God's redeeming love and gave us a vision for a healing path forward. I'm so thankful to both of you for doing your work and creating Faithful and True so that Greg and I and thousands of others could have a safe place to learn to walk a process of recovery and wholeness. You are a clarion voice for posttraumatic *growth*, and I'm grateful to work alongside you. More important, I'm thankful for your friendship.

And to the rest of the team at Faithful and True, you are such good people doing such good work. I'm thankful to be on the team, and grateful for your support of me in this.

To the hundreds of you I've met with in groups or individually, thank you for the privilege to come alongside in your pain and loss. You know that so many of these principles and ideas got fleshed out in our time together.

To those of you who allowed me to use your story to demonstrate what loss can teach us, my deepest thanks.

To my sweet boy, Winston, you were the recovery dog extraordinaire. Thank you for being such a harbor of joy and comfort in the middle of some tough storms.

To the ChiGonq Group, I'm so thankful we get to do life together as "framily." Greg and I might be the older generation of this framily unit, but that will probably only keep us young . . . so yet another reason I'm grateful for all of you.

Sheryl, Kristin, Karen, Carrie, Kelly, and Melissa, you are beautiful, strong feisty women who have loved me so well over the years on this journey and supported me specifically in the writing of this book. Framily, indeed.

Gramps, thanks for being so supportive. For all the many, many times you asked, "How's the book coming?" I'm grateful.

Mom, while you no longer have the words, history tells me that you would be supportive of me in this because of how you've encouraged me over the years. Thank you for the way you showed up for my family and helped keep our ship afloat.

Paul, thank you for being so encouraging of me in this process and your graciousness towards my writing about our family. For so many reasons, you're a really good big brother.

Jacob and Caleb, for your generous spirit towards me and the story of our family, I'm forever grateful. One of my deepest treasures is that you are my sons—and, now as adults, my friends. I'm so glad we've all been growing up together in one way or another. Time with you is always well spent. You truly bring me joy.

Greg, thank you for doing your work so that so many years later, we can sit in our kitchen and talk about our kids, our dog, or theology as we cook dinner. Sometimes it's the big life moments that prompt my awareness of how grateful I am that we're together, but more often it's the random Tuesday evening when I'm reminded of the simple goodness that we are each choosing to be well and choosing each other in the process. You have been such an encourager for me in this as in so many other things. Thank you for speaking truth to me to write from my voice—and then for reading every word once I did.

INTRODUCTION

I n my senior year of college, a friend of mine received the devastating news that her father had been involved in an ongoing affair for several years. To complicate matters, he was the senior pastor of a large church, and the affair partner was the spouse of a fellow staff member. Their experience was public and painful. While visiting my friend in her home that summer, I had a conversation with her mom about what had unfolded. Empathy welled up in me for sure, but so did something else I couldn't quite shake. My friend's mom would come to mind often over the years, and looking back, I have wondered if it was a premonition of sorts. In the summer of 2005, my own life exploded with the revelation of my husband's infidelity. At the time, we were both on staff at a large church. Ironically, he oversaw recovery and pastoral care ministries, and I led a ministry for hurting marriages. Our story was public and painful.

This isn't a book about why I stayed or why you should or shouldn't. (No one else can determine that for you anyway.) This is a book about the next layer down—the strangely wrapped gifts that come to us in the process of walking through loss, no matter the source, shape, or origin. Saint John of the Cross referred to it as a dark night of the soul. I can attest to the fact that I've experienced losses that are plenty dark. And yet, as Barbara Brown Taylor said, "New life starts in the dark. Whether it is a seed in the ground, a baby in the womb, or Jesus in the tomb, it starts in the dark."[1]

Being a good steward is one of God's many gifts. God truly wastes nothing and will often use the pain that comes our way in such dark nights to invite us into the process of more deeply knowing Divine

Love and better knowing ourselves. I've known many people who have experienced losses (of marital brokenness or other profound pain) who have chosen to just patch themselves up, put their heads down, and "get through it." And yet . . . what if our good, compassionate God longs for all of us to be on a formational journey toward our true selves and offers us an "on-ramp" to that experience through our pain? Agony is unique in the way it grabs our attention. Typically though, we just want to shut the pain down in the fastest way possible. I can own that I have many strategic, effective ways of numbing mine. On my better days, I'm learning that pain is almost always an invitation.

Maybe you're reading this and you're in the wake of a broken marriage, of losing a child to an accident, or of losing a spouse to cancer. Those losses are clear and definable. Losses can also be more subtle. Perhaps you're coming into awareness of your pain around something you haven't had (the support and blessing of a parent, an intimate marriage, or professional fulfillment). As I write this, we are in the midst of a pandemic that has been full of loss in slow motion as well as many sharp edges. Loss—in its many shapes and nuances—is a part of life, but thankfully, so are the invitations of growth it offers.

Years ago, our family was hiking in the mountains in Colorado. Rumor had it that a waterfall awaited us at the end of the trail, yet the ascent proved challenging with rocky trails, foggy weather, and a particularly large field of boulders. For a while we wondered if we would be able to cross the field. We made our way step by step through the massive rocks, but our choices of how to navigate the boulders were random. On the way back, I had a little higher view as we approached the field. What I hadn't seen from the other side—because I was either too overwhelmed or just not up high enough—was that a set of boulders were placed close together like steppingstones, forming a pathway. They provided a route less haphazard that made traversing the field easier. After walking my own journey of healing for the last fifteen years and walking alongside hundreds of others over the last ten, I can tell you: There is a path. It certainly isn't linear, but it is redemptive. What follows are several guide stones for being a good steward of your pain while saying yes to the invitation of growth *in* it. My path has also taken me on a journey of learning about spiritual practices that have proven to be meaningful building blocks for more deeply knowing God and myself. Several practices are included along the way as helpful companions.

To be clear, those who go through the agony of deep loss experience a season of triage in which they must tend to the open wounds and determine what's needed to move forward. Often, the first act of business is simply being heard and having our pain validated. It can actually do more harm than good to rush someone into prematurely looking at how God may be using his or her pain for good. In the early days of our explosion, I resonated with Wile E. Coyote who had been run over by a steamroller. I felt as two-dimensional as that cartoon character when I tried to peel myself off the ground. It takes a little while to start moving beyond that initial phase to becoming more "3D," capable of taking in a broader picture. If you are in the early stages of your own shattering loss, give yourself the space you need to breathe, and trust that you'll know when the time is right to consider the wisdom this loss has to offer. I'm also aware that the "steppingstones" in the following chapters are things I've been exposed to or have come to understand over the last several years. Embrace what seems like a good fit for you now—and what may be a vision for a few years down the road.

I am still amazed at the way my life has expanded since our crash and burn. Initially I was convinced it would be *the* thing that defined my life for the rest of my days. While I discover a need for another lap of grief every now and then, I'm more aware of my gratitude for the growth it has led to. That doesn't mean I'm thankful for what happened—or that God couldn't have used other means to form and shape me. It does mean that I'm in the process of learning to trust that God redeems all things. I pray you'll listen to the holy whispers of God as you find yourself at this juncture. May this be an on-ramp to the deeper journey of emotional and spiritual formation that will truly heal, transform, and shape the way you live and love. Seek to be open to what this loss can teach you, as counterintuitive as that may seem. In the words of C. S. Lewis, "Courage, dear heart."[2] New life really does begin in the dark.

ONE

Good Grief

What I once considered mutually exclusive—sorrow and joy, pain and pleasure, death and life—have become parts of a greater whole. My soul has been stretched.
—Jerry Sittser, *A Grace Disguised*

Grief touches us all. At different times of our lives, it finds each one of us—and we are often unprepared for its intensity and hesitant to plunge into its transformative depth.
—Alexandra Kennedy, *Honoring Grief*

In the days and months following my husband's public firing, the only thing I really wanted to do was curl into a fetal position and stay in bed. I've never been a morning person, but in the wake of our explosion I forced myself to put my feet on the ground quickly when I awoke for fear I'd never move if I didn't. For my boys, who were eight and eleven at the time, I wanted to maintain some semblance of normalcy. As chaotic as it was, one of the things they wanted to do was go to church. Due to the size of the church, their friends weren't aware of what was going on. Their leaders were kind and loving, so I leaned in. One Sunday in particular stands out in my mind as a microcosm of the chaos. I dropped the guys off at their groups and headed out to a nearby coffee shop (I didn't have the capacity to sit in a service). Traffic was often an issue, and orange cones were spread all over the parking lot to direct the cars as they came and went. While normally they were arranged in intentional patterns, that morning I came upon cones strewn in disarray as I tried to exit the church grounds. It was like some twisted obstacle course, and I unavoidably ran over a few on my way out. Without warning, this crazy anger bubbled up in me toward the *cones*. Words came spewing out of my mouth I didn't even know I knew. I was so off-the-charts angry at RIDICULOUS ORANGE CONES. As I pulled out onto the street, an awareness washed over me. I've lived a lot of my life in the South, so the voice in my head sounded something like this: *Oh honey, that's contempt.*

Of course, my anger wasn't about the cones. I had just become that parent who dropped her kids off at church and left (no doubt at some point in my life I had judged others who had done the same). My husband and I were separated after a very public explosion. He had been fired, and I was now the primary breadwinner for our family, employed by the church where it had all come to light. I couldn't see straight for the depth of my pain. Thankfully, a holy whisper rose up in me that morning. *This is contempt. Trust what you know: Contempt signals unprocessed grief. You are grieving. Of course, you are grieving.* I don't remember much else about that morning other than that I found my way to the coffee shop, parked far away from anyone else, and wept.

Having lived my life in largely Christian circles, emotions like contempt, bitterness, and resentment were usually only discussed in the context of things to avoid. I had come to believe that I was supposed to dodge those feelings or confess and/or squash them quickly like emotional Whack-A-Mole. Yet on closer inspection I began to understand that emotions themselves aren't right or wrong. We are made in the image of God (see Genesis 1:26-27); therefore, God must have emotions and has designed us with the capacity to have and feel them as well. That was new to me . . . the idea that God created us with the capacity to feel things like anger, resentment, contempt, disgust, or bitterness. The question is what we *do* with those emotions. While indulging and wallowing in them is detrimental, another option is that they have something to teach us. I like to think of afflictive emotions as warning lights that flash on the dashboard, letting me know something is amiss. As in "pay attention here . . . there's something deeper going on." Just like when the check engine light comes on in my car, it's not enough to simply notice. The issue needs to be examined and addressed.

When we "open the hood" and start looking around, often we find that unprocessed grief lies just underneath those layers of emotions like bitterness, contempt, resentment, or maybe even anxiety or fear. Grief, though, is one of the emotions we want to avoid the most, and we will go to great lengths to steel ourselves from feeling it for fear it will swallow us whole. As unpleasant as those other kinds of emotions can be, they somehow don't feel as unwieldy or unsafe as grief. We can find ourselves camping out in the woods of those "safer" emotions and not going any further. Understandably, especially in light of catastrophic loss, we fear that engaging our grief will cripple us. What is true, however, is that avoiding it takes far more energy and leads to a host of other issues. It's not as if we get to decide *I'm just not going to grieve this.* That unprocessed grief will go somewhere. "If we do not transform our pain," says Richard Rohr, "we will most assuredly transmit it—usually to those closest to us: our family, our neighbors, our co-workers, and, invariably, the most vulnerable, our children."[1] "Leaking out," it's often called. It's when we're snarky, sarcastic, irritable, unkind, bitter, contemptuous, frenetic, resentful, controlling, or even rage-filled toward another. It's a $100 reaction to a $10 issue. Rather than being centered down, we swirl like a Tasmanian devil. Rather than seeking to be present with ourselves and with Presence, we leak our pain onto those around us.

Grief will also affect our bodies, showing up in fatigue, an inability to concentrate, forgetfulness, appetite changes and/or digestive issues, aches and pains, headaches, tightness in the chest, or shortness of breath.[2] It's helpful to know what to look for so we know we're not crazy when our grief manifests itself in these ways. If those kinds of symptoms persist, it's wise to ask ourselves if we are avoiding feeling our pain so that our grief is "seeping in." The body doesn't lie and can be a barometer of our emotional health. Just as contempt or bitterness can be flashing lights on our dashboard, so can digestive issues or headaches that won't let up.

In *A Grace Disguised*, Jerry Sittser uses the term "second death" to describe what happens when we avoid leaning into our grief. At one point or another in this life, we will experience a "first death," whether that is the literal death of a loved one or a figurative death: struggling with health issues (ours or a loved one's); going through a divorce; experiencing the death of a dream about what we would do professionally or what our marriage would be like; suffering abuse or neglect as a child; or enduring loss from a natural disaster, assault, or a promise broken. "The destruction of the soul represents the tragedy of what I call the 'second death,'" Sittser writes, "and it can be a worse tragedy than the first. . . . [The second death] is the *death of the spirit*, the death that comes through guilt, regret, bitterness, hatred, immorality, and despair. The first kind of death happens *to* us; the second kind of death happens *in* us. It is a death we bring upon ourselves if we refuse to be transformed by the first."[5]

The "first deaths" that inevitably come our way in this lifetime are painful enough without a subsequent second death. So what does it look like to lean into the first one?

A Paradigm for Grief

A woman set an appointment with me to ask for help regarding her recent discovery of her husband's infidelity. She got right to the point: "I want my happy back—and tell me how to quickly get there." After communicating that her desire was understandable, I shared my belief that the route to happy was in moving through her grief, not around it. She never called back.

While no one grieves exactly the same, it can be helpful to have a big picture of what it looks like to "move through our grief." My dear friend and spiritual mentor, Sheryl Fleisher, introduced me to the concept of understanding grief through the paradigm of death, burial, and resurrection. It can be helpful to think of the phases of grief much like seasons of the year with their unique characteristics.

Death

The season of death is marked by a profound loss and such initial accompanying characteristics as shock and denial. Intensity and energy mark this phase, along with emotions that range wildly from a wave of sadness to anguish, despair, anger, and disbelief. A frequent rush of adrenalin can accompany this stage, depending on news we receive or greater realizations of what has been lost. Given the depth of emotion expressed, death is often experienced at high volume.

The weeks leading up to and immediately following the passing of my beloved father reflected this season well. About two years following a diagnosis of bile duct cancer and a massive surgery, Dad began to show signs that the cancer was returning. At the time, he was still the primary caregiver for my mother, who was dealing with her own increasing struggle with Alzheimer's. My brother, Paul, and I moved our mother into an assisted living home near the skilled nursing facility where Dad was being cared for in their hometown of Nashville. Paul was in Raleigh and I was in Chicago, and we commuted back and forth regularly that spring and summer to care for our parents. Doctors' appointments, decisions about hospice, navigating the transition with Mom, and long meaningful/hard/beautiful/difficult conversations filled our time. As strange as it sounds, a type of energy permeated those days that was simultaneously deeply painful and life-giving. My dad was relational to the core, and friends from across his life flew in, called, or stopped by regularly.

A few days before Dad died, Paul and I invited a host of our parents' friends to pack into his room for an old-fashioned hymn-sing. Strains of "Come Thou Fount" and "Blessed Assurance" filled the room and spread through the wing of the facility that afternoon. I watched as my dad closed his eyes and basked in the beauty of the voices. My mom was no longer able to understand that Dad was dying, yet she knew every word of those hymns—and for that afternoon it was enough. Later in the week, the energy shifted again. Many people talk about watching a loved one cross quietly to the other side. That was not our experience. Dad's final hours were marked by something called "air hunger" that left us beside ourselves with anguish. We wept and mourned that night as we said good-bye. We were shocked at how the end came, and I suppose we were shocked that it came at all, despite what we knew to be true. The energy of that season of death would turn again. And over the next week, we were buoyed by an outpouring of love and a celebration of a life well lived.

Burial

Just as seasons start to change, the season of my grief began to shift into less intensity over the next few months. Some days I felt so empty and adrift that I struggled to find any energy for being present with my grief (which honestly felt worse at times than the intensity from the prior months).

As I headed into a Chicago winter that year, the weather aligned with a time of "burial" I was experiencing that can be described as vacant, quiet, vulnerable, and lonely. My grief had fewer sharp edges but was still heavy as I tried to wrap my head around Dad's "gone-ness" and the truth that I was simultaneously losing my mother to Alzheimer's. Many days I felt muted, like a cold, gray winter's day. My emotions were less raw but still heavy and needed to be felt and moved through when possible. Things internally had started to settle down some, and I was often hesitant to revisit my grief that I knew was still very much with me.

Words from psychologist and author James Finley proved helpful during this season because they gave me permission to lean into my pain in bite-size pieces. "Move towards your suffering with love," he said, "and then back to the Source of Love."[4] Notice that the starting place is actually resting in the Source of Love (such a great name for God) because that's the place one comes *back to* after moving toward their pain. Resting in Divine Love allows me the capacity to move toward my pain as I am able, to acknowledge and feel it, and then to move back to the Source of Love. We were never designed to grieve solely out of our own strength.

Sometimes while I was in that season, however, praying (in a traditional sense at least) felt out of reach. A decade prior—in the loss with my husband—I had experienced something similar and found it disconcerting. I had never *not* been able to pray as I understood prayer at the time. But I had a comfy green chair that I would often just crawl into and say something like: *This is all I've got, God. I'm here.* I didn't have the awareness then that I was in burial. How comforting in my later years to discover it's understandable and even *biblical* to be in that place.

In *When the Heart Waits*, Sue Monk Kidd wrote that one day she was mulling over the story from Matthew 26 of Jesus and the disciples in the Garden of Gethsemane.

> Sit here while I pray . . .
> Sit here while I pray . . .
> Sit here while *I* pray . . .

She described being thunderstruck at a new understanding of that story: the idea that maybe, in certain seasons when we don't have words, what's needed is for us to simply sit while *God* prays. Which, as it turns out, is scriptural: "But if we hope for what we do not see, we wait for it with patience. Likewise the Spirit helps us in our weakness; for we do not know how to pray as we ought, but that very Spirit intercedes with sighs too deep for words" (Rom. 8:25-26).

"The emphasis isn't on what we're doing but on what God is doing," Kidd wrote. "Ultimately, we don't heal, transform, or create ourselves. We posture ourselves in ways that allow God to heal, transform, and create us. The posture of sitting while Jesus prays reminds us that the Spirit is active and speaking."[5]

I talk with people who have known great loss who find it alarming when they don't have any desire or motivation to pray. Often, they feel shame and fear that they are disappointing God. Maybe in this season, faithfulness looks like crawling into your version of a comfy green chair and allowing the Spirit to intercede on your behalf in a time of burial.

Resurrection

Years ago, the young daughter of one of my dearest friends came over to help me plant some bulbs. We bundled up that November morning, dug the openings, and covered the bulbs for their winter rest. Giving the dirt one final pat, we wished them well and said we'd look forward to seeing them in about six months. It's possible that I might whine a little about the length and depth of Chicago winters. But they somehow seem to encourage true appreciation for the awakening that comes in the spring, and that year was no exception. When purple flowers bloomed at the edge of my yard in May, I was reminded that new life really does start in the dark.

If we are faithful to grieve healthily the first deaths that come our way, resurrection will follow. Often that will require surrendering to a posture of being quiet and present with God while God is bringing about internal shifts. It's allowing the emotions to move through us when they bubble up, in small waves or larger swells. We begin to experience shades of hope and joy, more energy, and a new flow of love. It won't be linear (nowhere close). As with spring in Chicago, sometimes a cold snap will appear when we are confident winter has moved on. One year, in the middle of May, I watched in disbelief as snow piled up on the patio furniture that we had just moved to the deck a few days earlier, when it was 65 degrees and sunny. Similarly, a wave of grief may surprise us when we're convinced that we've passed through the deepest waters. That's part of the process, and it doesn't mean we are failing.

Resurrection will stir new life in our spirit and will often include shifts in our thinking, such as a new awareness or growth in our understanding of self, others, or God. Maybe what is being resurrected is our voice, self-compassion, a commitment to active recovery, our identity as a beloved child of God, or our willingness to let go more and more of our false self and embrace our true self.

Healthy grieving doesn't mean we will "get over" all of our losses. Certainly, we can grieve and move through many painful experiences, yet some will always be with us because of the depth of the hurt. Rather than "getting over" a catastrophic loss, we learn to make room for the flow of sadness that runs through us, like a tunnel we move through instead of a cave we wander around in aimlessly. After a season of rumbling, resurrection may result in freedom—or sorrowful acceptance of what is. Resurrection doesn't have to mean we will no longer feel sad; it may mean that, as emotionally and spiritually wise adults, we are learning to hold the seemingly opposite tension of our sorrow while embracing new life.

I have had the sacred privilege of hearing so many stories from people's lives in the last decade. I know that some losses are so profound that resurrection seems out of reach. And even then, in ways we didn't expect, God brings new life. Consider this story of resurrection of Jairus's daughter as paraphrased by author Sally Lloyd-Jones:

> *Jairus' servant rushed up to Jairus. "It's too late," he said breathlessly. "Your daughter is dead."*
>
> *Jesus turned to Jairus. "It's not too late," Jesus said. "Trust me."*
>
> *At Jairus' house, everyone was crying. But Jesus said, "I'm going to wake her up." Everyone laughed at him because they knew she was dead."*
>
> *Jesus walked into the little girl's bedroom. And there, lying in the corner, in the shadows, was the still little figure. Jesus sat on the bed and took her pale hand.*
>
> *"Honey, he said, "it's time to get up." And he reached down into death and gently brought the little girl back to life."[6]*

Sometimes resurrection looks like Jesus reaching down into the death of our spirit, hopes, dreams, family, friendships, or marriage and lovingly, firmly, telling us *it's time to get up*. And then ever so gently, bringing us back to life.

While it took me a little while to realize it, the emotional upheaval I experienced the day I ran over the orange cones was an invitation to truly engage *active grieving*, to say yes to the process of death, burial, and resurrection. While I had been working to be present with my pain, I could vacillate to running from it just as well. I was longing for "normal" and didn't want to journey with my grief for fear it would engulf me. I was (and still am) quite skilled at coming up with ways to numb and/or avoid my pain, such as busyness, work, TV, and eating. Thankfully, over time and with good help, I began to explore the invitation my emotions and reactions were offering.

In "death," I needed to sift through my grief, considering what this loss had cost me. I allowed myself to feel angry, to weep, mourn, and ride the waves of the shock and the intensity of the pain. Safe community provided a place for me to ask "why" about so many things.

In "burial," I was invited into the emptiness I experienced because of all that had died, and the vulnerability I felt as a result. I was encouraged to simply sit while God prayed, because nothing in me could. I was reminded that new life starts in quiet, dark places.

In "resurrection," I was challenged to move toward the riskiness of joy, gratitude, and hope that God—by some extraordinary alchemy—was redeeming my story. I was invited to consider that God wasn't just resurrecting my old life but was wanting to shape something in me that was altogether new, welcoming me into the wisdom this loss had for me. I was encouraged to see that sorrowful acceptance and wellness, even freedom in my soul, could co-exist. And that because Christ is the Resurrection, in whom I live and move and have my being, my grief would not be wasted.

Despite my bent toward avoiding it, that is good grief indeed.

Spiritual Practice: Creating a Healing "Sanctuary"

Often we may be open to journeying with our grief but unsure of what that might look like. Creating space to do so can take a few paths.

A. Spend some time creating an inviting space in your home that is to be a safe place for you to be present with your grief. Maybe it's a favorite chair, a place in your closet, or a corner of your laundry room. Bring into this space items that help you to exhale deeply: a candle, a journal, pictures of beauty, a few beloved books, a great blanket, and/or a way to listen to music. When in a season of deep grief, set aside time daily or weekly to be physically present in this space, which hopefully will lead to emotional and spiritual presence. The practice itself is helpful to begin cuing your body and soul that this is a time and space in which you can let down. Here are a few ground rules:

- Set a timer on your phone so you can trust that you have safe limits around the experience. If you want to go longer, feel free to, and if you need to stop sooner, listen to yourself well and do so. Start with as little as five minutes and try to increase the time and let it unfold.

- When you are present in this space, ask yourself *What do I need?* Consider some of these options:

  1. Journal
     — What you're sad about
     — What you're angry about
     — What losses you've experienced
     — Any concerns about what you're *not* feeling
     — The many ways this loss has impacted you
     — What fears are surfacing in you because of this loss

  2. Listen to music you find healing or that helps you access your sadness. Know that this is not the same as manufacturing emotion. Sometimes we've stuffed our emotions so far down that when we do seek to get in touch with them they seem unreachable. Music can be a pathway to invoke what is deep within us and needs to be expressed.

  3. Remember the visual of moving toward your suffering with love and then back to the Source of Love. Ask God for an image that represents how that can look for you.

  4. If you feel numb and empty, rest while God prays.

  5. Give yourself permission to move back into the rest of your day. This is the part most of us fear we won't be able to do, and yet we are actually more equipped than we realize. Spend some time in gratitude (if that's an honest emotion for you right now), thanking God for being Immanuel, God with Us, who is with you in this season. Gratitude often grounds us and helps us transition back to daily life.

  6. If creating a space indoors isn't meaningful, find an inviting place of beauty outside. Maybe it's on a favorite path at the local forest preserve or in a fishing boat on the lake. Try returning to the same spot to help cue yourself to be attentive to your grief.

B. While journeying with your grief can be very intentional, as in the practice just described, the "sanctuary" can also be within you as you move through the process organically. As a memory washes over you as you cook dinner or drive to work, you can welcome it (rather than push it away), put your hand on your heart, and say something like: Oh . . . I grieve the loss of _____. When the beauty of a sunset stirs your sadness, stop and allow yourself to feel your grief. Be present with it in the ebb and flow of the moment.

TWO

God as Midwife, Not Rescuer

There is really nothing more to say—except why. But since why is difficult to handle, one must take refuge in how.
                                        —Toni Morrison, *The Bluest Eye*

There is no place so protected and hidden where suffering can't find you. There is no place so painful that Love can't reach.

                              —James Finley, "The Spirituality of
                                        Trauma and Healing"

John and Elizabeth Edwards were names frequently heard in the media in 2008. John made a bid to run for president, and not long after, the truth came to light that he was involved in an extramarital affair that produced a child. In that same year, his wife, Elizabeth, learned her breast cancer had returned. It was that illness that took her life two years later. In a tribute to her the day she died, a previously taped interview aired of Elizabeth sharing honestly how her life experiences had affected her view of God. Edwards had lived through the loss of her sixteen-year-old son in a car accident and the public scrutiny of her husband's infidelity, and she was facing metastasized breast cancer that her doctors had run out of options for treating:

I had to reconcile the God I thought I had with facts I knew. So if I was going to have a God, it couldn't be an intervening God anymore. I couldn't pray anymore for good God to intervene, which means I can't pray for him to intervene in my cancer. Instead, the God that I came to accept is a God that promises salvation and enlightenment, and that's the God I live with now. It's not entirely the God I want, but it is the God I believe I have.[1]

These comments aren't the kind typically heard in church. Some people may even be uncomfortable reading them, yet the authenticity they represent is spot on. I have talked with many who feel lost and angry because of the seeming absence of God in their painful circumstances. Often questions about God's whereabouts go unvoiced, but nevertheless they reverberate in a person's mind and heart. *Where were you God? Why didn't you stop this? How could you not have intervened?* A blessed few of us grew up in homes or church cultures that invited us to question God. Many of us see questioning God as an irreverent lack of faith, and yet the wonderings or doubts either persist or are shoved into a mental corner.

The biblical story in John 11 of Lazarus's sisters' response to his death shows that questioning God has long been part of the human experience. The sisters, Mary and Martha, send word to Jesus that "the one he loves" is sick. They believe Jesus can save Lazarus from dying if he comes soon enough. But Jesus postpones his trip to their village of Bethany and arrives a few days after Lazarus dies. John reports, "When Martha heard that Jesus was coming, she went out to meet him, but Mary stayed at home" (John 11:20). One can't help but wonder if Mary's initial response to her hurt and confusion at Jesus' late arrival is her withdrawal from him. So Martha goes alone, and one wonders if her words to Jesus are about her faith, her anger, or some combination of both: "Lord, if you had been here my brother would not have died" (John 11:21).

Martha and Jesus have an important conversation, and Martha returns home and pulls Mary aside. "The Teacher is here," she says, "and is calling for you" (John 11:28). This time Mary goes quickly in response to Jesus' request, and her agony matches that of Martha's: *"Lord, if you had been here . . ."* (John 11:32).

Mary and Martha have a meaningful relationship with Jesus, and their great disappointment that he had failed to come more quickly is understandable. We know the rest of the story, but they only know that their brother is dead because Jesus hadn't intervened soon enough. It can only be speculation, but I wonder if Mary and Martha felt betrayed by Jesus, having believed that their relationship with him would protect them from pain.

Their frustration is echoed elsewhere in the scripture. Psalm 22:1-2 says: "My God, my God, why have you forsaken me? Why are you so far from helping me, from the words of my groaning? O my God, I cry by day but you do not answer; and by night, but find no rest." The strongest example yet is Jesus himself hanging on the cross and quoting the psalmist, "My God, my God, why have you forsaken me?" (Matt. 27:46). *Where were you? Why didn't you intervene sooner?*

———————

What if it is spiritually formative—*even necessary*—to voice these questions? In Mary, Martha, the psalmist, and Jesus, we have theologically sound examples that suggest that is true. Maybe it's an important passage to traverse on our faith journey. It's not as if God doesn't know that we have questions and doubts, yet we often fear being honest about them. A woman in one of my support groups, Vivian, shared about her struggle of doing just this. Her husband's sexual betrayal was quite painful and resulted in legal penalties for him. Understandably, she was shaken to her core. As she met with a spiritual mentor, though, and voiced the question of "Why has God forsaken me?" the mentor responded out of her own fear and began to quote scripture to Vivian about God's faithfulness. Vivian knew it wasn't safe to pursue that line of thought with her mentor—in fact she felt shamed for doing so—and the response shut her down until a year later when she found space in a safe community to give voice to those concerns.

In *Amazing Grace: A Vocabulary of Faith*, Kathleen Norris suggests that part of how we engage our faith is by recognizing that it is on a continuum that includes "belief, doubt, and sacred ambiguity."[2] It seems we often define the opposite of faith as uncertainty, which is a rather limited view. Could it be, instead, that the antithesis of faith is disengagement rather than questioning? Maybe the path of authentic faith is to grapple with our beliefs, our doubts, and our sacred ambiguity. *To ask the questions.*

"Why" is usually and understandably at the beginning of our questions. *Why didn't you intervene? Why did you allow this to happen? Why didn't you protect him/her/us/me?* It's certainly the most human place to start. While it is rare to get an answer, we ask because we need to make sense of the anguish. We desperately long for a logical explanation of the chaos. Part of what we may need to grieve is that the God we trusted allowed this heartache to come our way . . . or that we believed our relationship with God (or our image of God) would protect us from this kind of pain. Sadly, shortcuts really aren't an option. If we are angry, disillusioned, or even incredulous, asking *why* invites movement in our grief and eventually opens a dialogue with the God we are angry with. "Lament is the path that takes us to the place where we discover that there is no complete answer to pain and suffering, only Presence," writes Michael Card.[3]

In *When The Heart Waits*, Sue Monk Kidd asks, "How did we ever get the idea that God would supply us on demand with quick fixes, that God is merely a rescuer and not a midwife?"[4] Several years ago I stood watch with my friend as she labored on Christmas Eve to give birth to her daughter—who was apparently in no hurry since it was ten days after the due date. The midwife, Glenda, was such a calming presence throughout the night, wise in knowing when to suggest a new tactic for pain relief or offer a challenge when it was time to push. Glenda couldn't rescue my friend from that circumstance, but she could help her navigate childbirth with tender strength. The dictionary defines a midwife as "one who helps to produce or bring forth something."[5] The idea of God bringing forth something in us rather than simply rescuing us is seen throughout scripture. The narratives of Abraham, Sarah, Jacob, Esther, Jonah, Peter, the woman at the well, and the paralytic at the pool of Bethesda, to name a few, are all stories of God's birthing something new rather than rescuing.

If we are open to the idea that God really is more about midwifery than rescuing, then another helpful question is *what. What do you want to form and shape in me, God? What do you want me to let go of? To surrender? What part of me needs awakened? What part of my false self needs to be shed so my wise adult self can be more present? What in me do you want to heal? What in me do you want to birth?*

How grateful I am for wrestling, because it's the wrestling that usually brings deeper awareness of God and ourselves. For grief and pain to be navigated authentically—a process that always involves grappling—we must examine our current images of God. It may not be a pretty passage, but it's necessary. Do we see God as a catalog we call and order from? Or as a type of Santa Claus who provides things in response to our good behavior? Have we believed that if we followed the "rules," we could control our life (and God in the process) and keep hard things from coming our way? Have we believed that God shows God's love to us only through intervention? Have we believed that our relationship with God will protect us from painful experiences? Or have we believed that God is good if life is good, and thus a painful life means that God is absent, cruel, and has abandoned us? If we will respond to Jesus' invitation to wrestle, healthy grieving will lead us to a much more authentic view of God. "But what about you? . . . Who do you say I am?" (Matt. 16:15, NIV). It's a question we must each answer authentically and probably several different times throughout our lives as we're faced with how our view of God doesn't align with what we're experiencing.

Years ago, my beloved youth minister was diagnosed with leukemia and died at the young age of thirty-three. He was adored by our church and was like a brother to my dad, who was the pastor at the time. Losing Ron was a huge loss for so many. A few years later when I was in college, I was processing his death with some new friends as we sat in a car in the dorm parking lot. One of the guys in the car flippantly suggested that Ron died because he didn't have enough faith that God would heal him. At eighteen, I didn't quite have my theology worked out to articulate a wise response. I was angry and told him I didn't agree with that idea at all. I just knew in my gut that it didn't square with who I knew God to be. The way I remember it, I soon got out of the car and decided those weren't my people. In hindsight, I see that I recoiled from the suggestion that a system of simplistic explanation could be applied to Ron's illness, because I intuited that such explanations lack respect for the complexity and mystery of life in general and of God in particular. And I'm thankful that "my people" these days are comfortable with questions.

Martha is understandably focused on the individual story of her brother's death. When Jesus promises her that Lazarus will rise again, Martha seems to miss the point. Then Jesus becomes really clear: "I am the resurrection and the life. Those who believe in me, even though they die, will live" (John 11:25). Right here, in the middle of this story, Jesus draws Martha's attention to the larger story. More is happening than Martha can see, and Jesus is at work as a midwife, not a rescuer. He wants to birth something in her and in those gathered that is bigger than a quick fix.

As the story unfolds, Jesus interacts with Mary and is moved and troubled as he hears the mumbles of the crowd. The words in Greek here for "deeply troubled" can be translated as "angered." While it's only speculation, one wonders if Jesus weeps because the family and friends do not understand the bigger picture.

Jesus presses on, asking that the stone be rolled away, and prays: "Father I thank you for having heard me. I knew that you always hear me, but I have said this for the sake of the crowd standing here, so that they may believe that you sent me (John 11:41-42). *Midwife, not rescuer.*

As a midwife seeking to bring something forth, he calls forth Lazarus. "And the dead man came out" (John 11:44). And he calls forth Mary, Martha, and those desiring to listen: "I am the resurrection and the life. Those who believe in me, even though they die, will live, and everyone who lives and believes in me will never die" (John 11:25-26).

Sometimes God rescues. Jesus, Immanuel, *God with Us,* coming to us, is the most meaningful lens through which I understand God to rescue, and we do well to remember that as the fullness of the truth.

Yet God doesn't always intervene. And it's healthy for us to voice our feelings, doubts, and questions to God and about God with our safe people when God seems absent. While our feelings are our true feelings, it doesn't necessarily mean our feelings are *the* truth. But we start where we are, and sometimes where we are is disappointed, hurt, angry, disillusioned, or even incredulous. It is a faithful expression of our trust in God that God can handle our emotions (that God designed us to have).

And God doesn't always rescue, especially with quick fixes. Yet God is always about our good, wanting to birth in us the next layer of health, the next round of formation. I don't pretend to know why God chooses to allow some things to happen. This side of heaven, I imagine we will continue to live in the tension of the sovereignty of God and our freedom of choice—and how those two things intermingle to impact what happens in our lives. To be clear, I don't want to imply that God makes difficult things happen to us so that we can grow. What I know is that sometimes painful things happen and that "in all things God works for the good of those who love him" (Rom. 8:28, NIV). And sometimes that good can be difficult to see, so we rest (or rumble) in the sacred ambiguity of what new thing is being born.

Midwife, not rescuer.

Spiritual Practice: Dialogue Journaling

Dialogue Journaling is a type of journaling designed by spiritual director and author Helen Cepero in her book *Journaling as a Spiritual Practice.*[6] The exercise involves a written conversation with God that is truthful and unedited. Begin by writing your own name in your journal, followed by a colon. Without filters, honestly express to God how you feel right now. Put your pen down (or remove your hands from the keyboard) and listen. See what stirs. When you sense God responding, write a name for God followed by a colon, and then write what you sense God saying. Then pause and listen. What do you need to tell or ask God? Are there feelings of disappointment or anger you need to own? Are there some important "why" questions you need to ask God? Write, pause, and listen in dialogue fashion until you feel the conversation has ended for now. Sit in silence for a few minutes and be present with yourself and God. Seek to quiet any critical voices within that tell you this is ridiculous or can't happen. When you feel ready, use this practice to ask God questions that begin with "what." *What do you want to form and shape in me? What do you want me to let go of? What do you want me to know deep in my core?*

If you don't feel a dialogue develop during this exercise, notice if it opens something up in you later in the day or down the road.

THREE

Remain in My Love

*Define yourself radically as one beloved by God. This is the
true self. Every other identity is illusion.*
                                    —Brennan Manning, *Abba's Child*

*For we have known and believe the love that God has for
us.*

                                    —1 John 4:16

From the time I was young, my dad and I would often talk theology. He would share his point of view and was open to what I thought as well. In hindsight, I now realize how formative that was for a daughter to be engaged in those kinds of conversations with her father. A few months before he died, he and I were discussing his seminary training. "We were taught a fairly simple preaching formula," he explained. "Tell people how bad they were, how good God is, and how to bridge the gap from human depravity to God's goodness."

My eyes flew open as he finished his sentence. "Dad!! OH MY GOODNESS! First, I can't tell you how much I disagree with that, and second, this explains so much and validates my reality of what I experienced growing up in an evangelical culture!" He was used to my getting riled up, and quietly asked, "So then what do you believe?"

I began to share that over the last several years I had come to get a taste of belovedness. That while, yes, we can make poor choices, our ultimate identity is that we are first and foremost deeply loved. Our reality is one of *blessing*: We are loved. Period. Nothing can cause us to be more or less loved by God. We are simply and completely loved.

"And, Dad, here's the thing. You and mom never parented Paul and me in the way you're describing God. You never started with telling us how bad we were. You communicated that we were loved, wanted, delighted in. Yes, we didn't always make wise choices and there were consequences as a result, but it never changed your love for us."

He got quiet and teary and looked a little bewildered. "No," he said softly, "I can't imagine telling you and Paul how bad you were." He truly seemed unsure of how to reconcile the implications of what I was saying.

"How much more could God love us?" I asked him quietly. *How much more so God?*

In the context of deep pain and loss, how we see ourselves, how we see God, and the connection between the two are crucial. Pain often sends us reeling, questioning ourselves, God, or both. When our loss is one of not being chosen or cherished, we can begin to question our own lovability. When someone or something is taken from us, or when we long for something good that we don't have, we may question God and God's goodness. We can't imagine how a good and loving God is congruent with our reality. And with a deeper look, we often discover that present-day pain somehow highlights old core beliefs about ourselves and about God.

When we don't live our lives from a core belief of blessing, we instead believe that our identity is grounded in the unstable sand of our own actions, good or bad. We are lulled into thinking that making the right choices/living a good life/checking all the boxes can win God's "favor" and keep difficult things at bay. This may not even be conscious, but it will float to the surface when difficult things happen. Inevitably, our carefully constructed façade comes crashing down: a child dies of cancer, a spouse is unfaithful, we lose the baby. Maybe it's not one big thing like that, but we awake one morning to the realization of just how disappointed we are with our lives. Either way, we are left standing in disbelief, wondering, *How did I lose God's grace?* or *What kind of God allows this?* Maybe our lives are in shambles because of painful choices we have made. We are convinced that God is angry and that we've disqualified ourselves from being worthy of love. As David Benner writes, "What a small god we would have if divine character was dependent on our behavior."[1] Granted, poor choices have consequences. Yet blessing is constant. When we don't have blessing as our foundation, we allow the shifting sands underneath us to define who we are and how we see God.

I remember the first time I time I was encouraged to explore what I truly believed about God and how God saw me. I was a part of a small group in college in which the provost, Dr. Bill Hull, asked each of us to write our story. "What's the narrative you live by?" he challenged us to consider. "Not what you have been taught or think that I want to hear. Go the next layer down. What's the tape you actually listen to?"

I grew up in a church culture in which we were encouraged to *do* for God. Offering envelopes had boxes to check if you had done the "right things" for God that week.

> Read my Bible daily: *check*
> Gave to the church: *check*
> Visited the sick: *check*
> Prayed daily: *check*
> Brought my Bible to church: *check*

Annually there would be a missions offering, and each year would have a special theme. One year, a banner stretched across the balcony of our church with the slogan (no joke): *Do Something!* Offering envelopes and mission themes were shorthand for the narrative that unfolded for me: I had to hustle for God. I heard messages that told me God was love and that God loved me (*For God so loved the world*), but the grace of blessing wasn't the narrative I was surrounded by in church. It created cognitive and emotional dissonance.

While I grew up singing and hearing about grace in my conservative evangelical circles, it was most often in the context of it saving a "wretch like me." I see clearly now that it was presented from the starting point of how bad I was, how good God is, and the need to get from one to the other. As I ponder this now, I see that one of the "benefits" of this paradigm is allowing people to believe that they are in control of following the rules to get to God. I wonder if we're actually afraid of trusting that we are truly beloved, that what's most amazing about grace is that it *begins* with a blessing over which we have no control.

Blessing is the truth that I am unconditionally loved. It's knowing that God is *delighted* by me. So often we are taught or somehow come to believe that it's likely that God is disappointed, angry, disinterested, sad, or frustrated when we come to mind. We think God's view of us is based on our behavior. Blessing, however, is unconditional. There is nothing we can do to lose God's love or earn more of it. "For I am convinced that neither death, nor life, nor angels, nor rulers, nor things present, nor things to come, nor powers, nor height, nor depth, nor anything else in all creation, will be able to separate us from the love of God in Christ Jesus our Lord" (Rom. 8:38-39). That's our *origin*, but rarely is it our *origin story*.

In college, thanks to Dr. Hull, I began exploring the narrative I lived by, my origin story. It's a journey I'm still on—and in that process have found the words of Sue Monk Kidd so encouraging: "For always, always, we are waking up and then waking up some more."[2] What I've been awakening to is the awareness that my origin stories are varied and complex. I was raised by two loving parents, and my brother and I often felt loved and supported. But out of their own pain and origin stories, they didn't always know how to relate to one another, which created some emotional chaos in our home. My mom struggled with trauma from her family of origin that was never really treated and resulted in depression. From an early age, I often took on the role of caring for her emotionally. Out of those experiences, I developed the core belief that it was my responsibility to ensure the happiness of those around me. And given some of the messages I was taking in about God, I believed it was my job to please God as well. My worth and value became dependent on it. "When we struggle to believe in our worthiness, we hustle for it," writes Brené Brown. And "the hustle for worthiness has its own soundtrack and . . . it's not the funky 'do the Hustle' from the '70s."[3] For me, the soundtrack was this: perform, be responsible, and make sure everyone around you is okay.

As I continue to "wake up some more" to the narrative I've lived by, I'm coming to understand that all of us have wounds from things that have happened to us that we didn't need (defined as invasion) as well as pain from not receiving things we needed but didn't get (understood as abandonment). Sexual, physical, or emotional abuse; serious illnesses; and car accidents are types of invasion. Some examples of abandonment are being in a family where there is a favored child or a child with special needs, being raised by an emotionally absent parent, or being frequently left out and excluded by peers. Heartache has found all of us one way or another and has left its mark. The worst of the pain impacts how we see ourselves, our value, worth, and identity. In the middle of the night—or even in the bright of day—we hear those shaming and chaotic messages: *What's wrong with me, surely there is more to this life, I'm so screwed up*, or *this isn't what I signed up for.* These messages are often so loud we miss the original message that was there all along: "We are intimately loved long before our parents, teachers, spouses, children, and friends loved or wounded us. That's the truth of our lives. That's the truth I want you to claim for yourself. That's the truth spoken by the voice that says, 'You are my Beloved.'"[4]

Years ago, my friend and mentor Sheryl was leading me through a spiritual practice of imaginative prayer. I had been around the things of God my whole life, but as I began to be exposed to a more contemplative spirituality, I knew in my core that I didn't understand what it meant to *be* with God. Remember, "Do Something!" had been my mantra.

As we invited the God of all Creation to breathe a creative spirit into our prayer time, I began to allow my heart and mind to wander. With my internal eye, I saw myself as a four-year-old girl, standing in my childhood home. Jesus was there as well and invited me to walk down the street to the neighbor's pond. Hand in hand, we strolled down Silver Avenue. We found a little rowboat and climbed in. We rowed out to the middle of the pond, laughing and talking (I think my four-year-old little girl was kind of a chatterbox).

Almost twenty years later, I'm still deeply stirred at the movement that occurred in my soul that afternoon. First, I experienced Jesus looking at me with pride, joy, and delight. *Sheer delight.* He was smiling and happy—and I soaked in the truth that I was the object of that joy. But that wasn't all. In the beauty and creativity that is fostered in imaginative prayer, the viewpoint changed. I found myself sitting where Jesus was, watching my four-year-old self. I could see that she was, in fact, delightful. And again, something deep within shifted . . . away from doing, toward being. Away from striving, toward blessing. Before I left that side of the rowboat, the Spirit brought a final awareness. This time, it was me as a mother, with my own little boys, Jacob and Caleb, sitting across from me in the rowboat. Immediately I saw the significance of God's allowing me that perspective layered onto these two others: God knew that my love for my sons is such a part of my being that if I was reminded of my love for them that maybe, just maybe, I could catch a glimpse of how God sees me. *How much more so God?* "Behold God beholding you . . . and smiling," writes Anthony de Mello, SJ.[5] This is the picture of blessing, of belovedness. Knowing and experiencing the truth that when we come to God's mind, God *smiles.*

Once I was hosting a guest speaker at the church where I was on staff. I gave the usual "bio" type of introduction for the gentleman, and then I asked him if there was anything else he'd like us to know about him. "Yes," he said, without hesitation. "I'm a beloved son of God." I remember being drawn to the profound simplicity of that statement. It was obvious he was getting a taste of belovedness. And I was taken with how deeply, simply, and clearly he knew it.

The temptation is to ask, "How do I *do* this? "Recognizing that we are wholly acceptable is God's own truth for us—waiting to be discovered," writes Gregory Boyle.[6] This isn't something we do, achieve, or perform. It's something we say *yes* to. *It's already true.* Scripture tells us that God referred to Jesus as his "Beloved" and that Jesus loves us in the same way: "As the Father has loved me, so I have loved you; abide in my love" (John 15:9).

It's true that we are beloved—and also true is that we are prone to wander. It's why Jesus encourages us to abide, to remain in his love.

The parable of the loving father and two sons is a beautiful story of a father's radical love for his children who were prone to wander. Many times I've heard a sermon on this parable, often with the question "Which son are you more like?" posed at the end. The implication is that we either leave God by heading to the far country of wild living or we stick around and get resentful. I wonder if there is wisdom in seeing how we are related to both of these brothers.

When my life crashed and burned, one of the strangely wrapped gifts that came to me was the discovery of just how much of my identity had been firmly rooted in what others thought of me and how I could perform. (And no, that didn't feel much like a gift at first.) My far country might not have been "wild living" but rather image management and searching for my worth. I was "leaving home" and looking for a sense of security in my marriage, my intact family, and how others perceived me as a leader. When all of those things were shaken, it left me scrambling for solid ground. It makes perfect sense for us to want a healthy marriage, a cohesive family, and respect. Yet we don't find our center of gravity in things that can be taken from us due to our actions or those of others. We find it in the unchanging love of God.

Any time I leave the "home" of God's blessing in search of my well-being, I am the younger sibling. I can wander by seeking someone else's approval, pursuing achievement, or attempting to control what's happening around me. In *Return of the Prodigal Son*, Henri Nouwen writes, "I am the prodigal son every time I search for unconditional love where it cannot be found. Why do I keep ignoring the place of true love and persist in looking for it elsewhere?"[7]

Equally painful *and* freeing is the realization that I am also the older brother. The older brother struggled when his father threw a party for the returning son. He was resentful that the younger brother was getting celebrated when he was the one who had stuck around. He missed the truth that the relationship with the father *was the party all along.* He had tried to do life perfectly as a means of control, and when his "goodness" didn't seem to pay off, "his inner complaint paralyzed him and let the darkness engulf him."[8] He was prone to wander but into the darker places of his "inner complaint." Either way, both were far from home.

For most of us, it's counterintuitive that God's love really isn't something we have to earn. We are, in fact, beloved, and the invitation is simply to remain in it, to say yes to it, over and over again. So how do we say yes? First, we must allow ourselves time alone with God to sit in this truth. It's not a quick process. It's a slow surrender to regularly sitting in silence and solitude, listening for the voice of God that speaks the truth that we are loved. We ask God, *What do you want me to know about how you see me?* And then we listen. We picture ourselves entering into the Gospel stories: seeing ourselves as a child sitting on Jesus' knee or coming to him as one who has been sick with an illness for years, reaching out for the hem of his garment. And then we watch how Jesus responds to us.

We learn that when we get triggered into believing something else, we can give ourselves a reality check about where we have been prone to wander. For example, when we feel hurt, left out, angry, or betrayed, it's easy to attach meanings to those feelings: *I'm not enough, I'm too much, I don't measure up, I'm not* [smart, skinny, desirable, attractive, prosperous, successful, lovable, strong, powerful] *enough*. But just because we make meanings out of something doesn't at all guarantee that we've made a *true* meaning. We can have stories in our head about things that are informed by our filters (filters about God, ourselves, others, how we believe we fit in or don't). Even though those messages may be strong—and have probably been with us for a long time—it doesn't mean they're true.

Instead, we can begin to name what is: *I am a beloved child of God.* While we don't have to earn God's love, we will likely need to practice saying yes to it. Even (and especially) when we don't feel it, it's still true. We may at times feel rejected or abandoned, but that doesn't have to be *the truth* about us, despite how intense those feelings are.

Most of us don't come naturally to an understanding that we are beloved. Awakening to the truth of God's blessing on our life is an area that often requires healing, because life's circumstances and experiences have worked hard to tell us otherwise. I often hear stories from adults who were told by their parents (in childhood or even on into adulthood) that they were a disappointment. One man I knew was nicknamed "Zero" as a child. So many of us have experiences of learning that our worth is connected to how we perform, keep the peace, or make others happy. Even though they aren't true, messages like these form core beliefs in us that we end up building our sense of self around. Worse (yet understandably), we find it nearly impossible to take in that God would think differently.

We don't simply awake one morning and find we are finished with making unhealthy meanings. We listen for the Spirit of Truth speaking truth to our hearts, we remind ourselves that we are beloved, and we receive others' words of blessing to us. "Practice makes pathways," writes Danielle Shroyer.[9] In other words, as I practice reality-checking my false core beliefs, I am forging a new pathway in my heart and mind that allows me to live into saying yes to my belovedness. Scripture and science both support this truth. Science tells us that the brain has neuroplasticity and can rewire itself to learn new things. Scripture tells us, "See, I am making all things new" (Rev. 21:5) and "We have come to know and believe the love that God has for us" (1 John 4:16, ESV). We are set up from every angle to be able to shed false core beliefs and embrace the truth that we are beloved children of God. Just as fish cannot drown in water, we cannot change the truth that we are beloved. It is our nature—and this journey invites us to live within that nature rather than scrambling for our worth outside of it.

This journey will also call us to surround ourselves with others who can remind us of our truth, as we remind them. One of my favorite definitions of being triggered was coined by my husband, Greg. Being triggered means that we are knocked out of our truth. I regularly encourage those in the support groups I lead to reach out to group members to help them get back in the truth when they are triggered. It's a beautiful thing when someone is courageously vulnerable enough to do so. One woman told me that in a moment of wanting to believe the message of her old core beliefs, she decided instead to practice this new pathway and reach out to her group via text. "I'm struggling today," she wrote. "There are some really loud thoughts in my head about my unworthiness that are so familiar. I'm really tempted to believe them. Can you remind me of what's true?" The texts started to pour in:

> *You are beloved by God.*
> *You are enough.*
> *You don't have to hustle for your worth.*
> *I know this is hard. You're not alone.*

We often need community to remind us of the way back home.

———

Finally, an additional way we say yes to our belovedness is found in another truth from the story of the loving father and the two sons. David Benner writes, "The point of the spiritual journey is not simply to be received back into the welcoming arms of love of the Father but to become like the Father . . . If we are not becoming more loving, something is seriously wrong."[10] And that's the ultimate goal. As we remain in God's love and say yes to our own belovedness, we in turn become more loving. Maybe that's in a more tender and gracious understanding of how we relate to ourselves. Maybe it's in a more generous way we seek to understand another. Perhaps a crucial takeaway from that parable isn't only how we resemble both of the brothers; it's considering how we are growing in our capacity to resemble the father. Only in the upside-down kingdom of God would God ever so gently use our pain as an invitation to transform how we love. And what an invitation it is: to realize that we have a loving Parent waiting to embrace us, who invites us to do the same with others.

So I ask you the same question I was asked in college: What's the narrative you live by? What's your origin story? Could the pain of this season invite you into "waking up and then waking up some more" as you find your way into shedding false core beliefs about yourself or God? Just maybe there is a more accurate story:

> *How beloved we are by God*
> *How good God is*

And the truth that God is always moving toward us in Perfect Love,
inviting us to live within our nature and say yes to our belovedness.

That seems like a really good preaching formula to me. I think my dad
would agree.

Spiritual Practice: Imaginative Prayer

This journey of saying yes to our belovedness is deeply encouraged by
sitting with Jesus and listening to what Jesus has to say about us. The gift
of imaginative prayer is a type of "prayerful daydreaming" that allows
room for sacred movement within our souls. When we reflect on stories
from the Gospels, it's meditating on Jesus—imagining his movements,
words, facial expressions, compassion, and interactions with us. Prayer
unfolds as we "live into" a biblical story or scene with our imagination.

Begin by asking our creative God to lead and guide you as you pray
into one of these passages. Enter into a Gospel story of Jesus engaging
a person or a group—the sights, sounds, smells, feelings, and/or tastes.
Maybe you smell the fishiness of the sea, or you feel the heat of the day
bearing down on you. Allow yourself to imagine being present in the
scene and see with whom you identify. Or simply allow yourself to be in
the setting and notice what happens. Listen to see if Jesus has a word for
you (about the truth of your belovedness or anything else). Notice if you
have questions for Jesus.

Consider using one of these Gospel stories or another that comes to
mind. Attune to one you're drawn to and then read the passage, allowing the Spirit to lead as your mind wanders and your imagination flows.

- The woman who had been bleeding for twelve years (Mark 5:25-34)
- The paralytic at the pool of Bethesda (John 5:1-13)
- The disciples in the boat facing a huge storm (Mark 6:45-52)
- Jesus blessing the little children (Mark 10:13-16)
- Jesus and the man lowered through the roof by friends (Luke 5:17-26)
- The woman who had been crippled for eighteen years (Luke 13:10-17)
- Jesus healing the blind man (Mark 8:22-26)

FOUR

It's a Both/And

It is good that you should take hold of the one, without letting go of the other.

—Ecclesiastes 7:18

So, this is my life. And I want you to know that I am both happy and sad and I'm still trying to figure out how that could be.

—Stephen Chbosky, *The Perks of Being a Wallflower*

I can be angry about suffering. I can be thankful for deliverance. I can be both

—Miroslav Volf, *The End of Memory*

About a year into our journey, I found myself in a quandary. I was experiencing Greg in ways that were encouraging and hopeful. He was open, tender-hearted, and far more present with me and our kids. He was actively engaged in recovery because he was internally motivated, not because I was asking him to be. About the time I'd want to begin trusting that new behavior, this deafeningly loud voice would race to the forefront on my mind: *He betrayed you. He was deceptive. He's hurt you and others. How can you believe anything? Don't be a fool!* I was talking with a counselor one day during that season, explaining this bind I was experiencing. "I'm just not sure which of these things to hold on to," I told her. "This is so chaotic."

"What if it's both?" she said. "What if *all* of that is true? Your work will be to hold both of these truths and live in the tension of them." I knew it was wise counsel by the way her words landed in me. To move through this with either/or thinking wasn't going to give me the space I needed to navigate the whole of it.

As I began to sift through my awarenesses from both sides, I looked at what I was seeing in Greg. Often, grave consequences will bring about a deep desire for change, and this was no exception. From the beginning, Greg had been open and willing to take ownership for how he had hurt me and others by his actions, while doing the hard work of getting underneath the *why* of how things had unfolded. He was exploring the root causes of the pain he had tried to medicate with his behaviors and the false core beliefs he held that led to such painful choices. He was making good contributions to becoming a trustworthy person. *And* equally weighty was the truth that I had been deeply hurt. He had been unfaithful and dishonest to me and others. I knew it wasn't safe or healthy to rush back in. Taking time to acknowledge the wounds caused by his actions honored my dignity and validated my reality.

To cling to the awareness that Greg was recovering and healing was true—but not the fullness of the truth. If I only held to that, I would abandon the need to advocate for myself while holding a boundary that says that what happened is absolutely not okay. On the other hand, if all I was willing to see was how much I'd been hurt, it would prevent me from experiencing the fact that Greg was healing and that our marriage could possibly be reconciled. It would also interfere with my own need to explore some things for my emotional health. I would have to learn to live in the tension of seemingly opposite realities. Black-and-white thinking didn't leave room for this kind of paradox. I had to discover what it meant to think in the gray.

As children we need the concrete. Kids learn the meaning of short when compared with tall. Hot starts to makes sense when related with cold. When we are young, we think dualistically. If you've ever tried helping a three-year-old understand "Play time is fun *and* rest is needed to give you the energy to play," you know that level of reasoning rarely if ever gets an overtired toddler to settle down for a nap. Developmentally, it's not what a young child is capable of.

Yet, this is one of those places in which we are invited to "grow up into all things." We may still be using the framework we used as children if we haven't pushed through to both/and thinking. It's not that we need to rid ourselves of dualistic thinking; we need it to operate in our daily lives. I turn right or left at the corner, not both. My dishwasher is on or off; it can't be some combination of those two things. Yet we run into trouble if that's our only framework. It doesn't provide the necessary infrastructure to process the larger experiences in life, such as suffering, loss, or even love. It simply isn't substantial or accommodating enough.

If, for instance, I face suffering and loss with an either/or mentality, I'm likely to be short-sighted. It sets me up to think that God is present or absent, someone that hurt me is safe or unsafe, or that I (depending on my choices or actions) am good or bad. That doesn't leave much room to explore other possibilities. In fact, it often leads to dead ends. When dualistic thinking has the last word, we will find it challenging, for example, to consider the possibility of how God could be good and trustworthy when something painful has occurred. Because this hard thing happened, we reason, God didn't show up. End of story. We don't stretch ourselves into reframing our understanding that God was present in other ways while surrendering to the mystery of not knowing why God didn't move in the way we had hoped.

Rarely is the fullness of the truth either/or.

Once at a workshop, I was discussing the construct of the both/and when a participant pulled me aside at a break and asked: "What is the theological support for such an idea? What verse or passage are you basing this on?" Based on the energy with which he was asking the question, I sensed he didn't have much of an "appetite for paradox," as I've heard some refer to it, so I treaded lightly. It can be scary when we are challenged to question our infrastructure.

I shared how I was coming to see that rather than being either/or, God is both/and:

Human and divine
One and three

Tender and strong
Just and merciful
Present and future
Beginning and end

He gave me a quiet "Hmm," and walked away.

Let's be honest. This isn't anything we readily embrace. We try to dodge situations that offend our reason with carefully constructed rules, roles, or ways we believe we can cut off pain at the pass. And then the unthinkable happens: The house catches fire, a spouse dies far too young, you're sexually assaulted by someone you trusted, you develop a difficult to treat autoimmune disease. Loss and pain are truly offensive to our sense of reason; intense levels of pain make absolutely no sense. In an attempt to find reason in it, we scramble to reach for logic:

I wasn't enough to keep her from being unfaithful.
God is weak or uncaring and didn't intervene.
If I had been a better child, my dad wouldn't have left.
God needed another angel.
I need to ramp-up control so this will never happen again.

Our grasping for logic in the face of the illogical is understandable. We long to make sense out of the absurd in our lives because of our bias for logic and the "safety" that the structure of rationality provides. But the conclusions we draw are rarely helpful (or truthful), because the situation itself defies logic. It's like the urge to slam on the brakes when you're skidding on ice. Given the level of panic you feel when your car is careening, it seems logical but only makes it worse. The wiser choice is to surrender to the chaos of the slide.

———

Pain, loss, suffering, grief, and even *love*—the experiences in our lives that defy reason—will require something other than either/or thinking or a logical, rational approach. It's simply not large enough to hold any of these messier, complex, beautiful, mysterious aspects of being human. Carl Jung said, "Paradox is one of our most valued spiritual possessions."[1]

Defined as seemingly absurd yet really true, *paradox* comes from the two Greek words *para*, meaning "contrary to," and *doxa*, meaning "opinion."[2] Paradoxes are those situations/experiences/people/beliefs/ideas in life that hold two truths that, at first glance, seem incongruent.

In the midst of our loss, why does this matter? Because being willing to live into the both/and is a more accurate picture of the truth. And Jesus tells us that when we know the truth, it will make us free (see John 8:32). The reverse is also true: If I'm not living in the fullness of the truth, then I'm enslaved to just one aspect of it. I can't live as a wise adult grounded in reality if I am only willing to see one side or apply either/or thinking to a situation that requires much more of my mind and soul. To release our grasp on either/or and learn to hold the both/and will require trusting that there's more to an experience, a situation, or a person (ourselves included) than we could see at first glance. And some experiences will invite us further into mystery. We tend not to like mystery—as least not as a spiritual practice. We might be drawn to it when we know it will be solved at the end of an hour-long fictional crime drama, but not having answers to our deepest questions or reasons for our most profound pain feels scary and out of control. And there's the rub. Our pain reminds us that we aren't in control and can't figure out how to tie things up neatly. We long for certainty in the face of mystery, answers in the midst of questions.

The nature of divinity itself is mysterious. Divine and human, one and three, beginning and end, present and future: We may have a glimpse of who God is, but we can't with certainty know fully. Mystery, then, asks for surrender. Surrender to the truth that we only see dimly now and will one day see more clearly.

Surrender to the mystery of God.

Surrender to the truth that we may never be able to fully understand some of what occurs in our lives.

Surrender to the idea that if we are made in the image of the Divine, we ourselves are a mystery. We are a both/and. And to be Christlike, we are invited to embrace that mystery.

———

My great niece is the first baby of the next generation in our family. Pictures of her are regularly sent to the delight of the grandparents, aunts, and uncles. Milestones are reported with gusto: "She rolled over!" "She's pulling up!" "Look—she's taking a few steps!" With love and enthusiasm, I watch as the youngest member of our family grows and matures. Just as she has developmental stages she must reach physically, we have developmental stages to move through in becoming emotionally and spiritually healthy adults. A person's capacity to live in the tension of seemingly opposite realities is one of those stages. If we come up against inner conflicts or unanswered questions and aren't willing to meet those with expansive thinking, we stay stuck in a childish place of our emotional development. "Only the spacious, contemplative mind can see so broadly and trust so deeply," writes Richard Rohr. "The small calculating mind wants either or, win or lose, good or bad."[3] When children don't progress in developmental stages, it's referred to as "failure to thrive." Maybe that's what happens to us if we get stuck in small, calculating places in our thinking.

Wouldn't it be great if our friends and family began to see growth in us and would celebrate our milestones?

Did you see that?! She's thinking in the both/and not just the either/or!

He's willing to name he has some theological contradictions and that's okay!

She's starting to surrender to the mystery that maybe there is no clear answer for what happened!

He's getting less comfortable with systems of belief that want to tie things up neatly and don't allow for questions!

My friend Gerry was one of the people I've watched live out the paradigm of the both/and. In 2014, Gerry was diagnosed with pancreatic cancer after already having beaten breast cancer ten years prior. By Christmas of 2016, those of us in her community were heartbroken by the reality that Gerry was not long for this world.

On a bright, cold Saturday morning in December of that year, about five weeks before she died, I was at a brunch with Gerry and several other women. It was a rich time of community and friendship. From the beginning, the morning was distinctive, with many of us in a heightened state of awareness of the gift of being with Gerry, while trying to hold the tension of our ever-growing sadness about her illness. At some point, the conversation turned to a discussion of heaven in which we talked about a definition of heaven as both *here and now* and *there and then*. We listened to Gerry name how she had been experiencing heaven here and now in the expressions of love and care from her husband, Mel, and daughter, Melanie, and in the outpouring of support she had felt from so many. "Here this morning, around the table with each of you," she said. "The longevity of our friendships. All that we've been through with each other. This is heaven." Later I checked in with others who had been at the brunch. There was a consensus that we had been in a sacred, thin space that morning. That place where earth and heaven blur together for a time and you know you've been on holy ground.

Often, I've thought of that definition of heaven: *here and now* and *there and then*. I've never resonated with the perception that we don't belong here and that we are just biding our time until we get to heaven. It seems to me that we must trust that the Loving God who designed us to be on this earth had something good in mind for us here and now until the time God calls us home there and then. While we long for complete joy, total freedom, and perfect love in heaven, I believe a good measure of each of those is available to us presently.

Jesus often talked about the kingdom of God and the kingdom of heaven interchangeably—and spoke of them being here and now. Once Jesus was asked by the Pharisees when the kingdom of God was coming, and he answered, "The kingdom of God is not coming with things that can be observed; nor will they say, 'Look, here it is!' or 'There it is!' For, in fact, the kingdom of God is among you" (Luke 17:20-21). He taught us to pray: "Your kingdom come. Your will be done on earth as it is in heaven" (Matt. 6:10). Heaven, *here and now* and *there and then*.

It's understandable that we'd rather cling to a black-and-white understanding of heaven when what's here and now is grief-filled and difficult. To know my friend Gerry was to know that she was a believer in the both/and . . . that something didn't have to be black and white;

in fact, it hardly ever was. "It's a both/and," Gerry would often say. "It almost always is."

We need the both/and. The construct of paradox allows us to live with things that transcend understanding. According to Carl Jung, "only the paradox comes anywhere near to comprehending the fulness of life."[4] Remember, by its very definition, paradox is "seemingly absurd yet really true."

I don't understand why this painful thing has happened, and I am learning to surrender into the mystery of not needing a logical way to explain it all.

I can learn to see that others are not all bad or all good—and neither am I.

I can feel sadness and have space for joy. In fact, the former makes room for the latter.

I may have had the faith that God could have intervened, and I can trust (or learn to trust) that God is good even if God didn't.

Just as pain and suffering require mystery, so does love. Love, in its simplicity and complexity, somehow covers a multitude of sins—ours and everyone else's. Love allows us the courage to see that we ourselves are a both/and, a beautiful, chaotic mix of goodness *and* capacity to wound another. Love allows us the courage to know that others are a both/and as well. We will be hurt, wounded—*and* forgiveness is possible. Healing can happen, and sometimes, thankfully, relationships are restored. Love allows us to move toward another *and* hold boundaries when necessary.

We have come from Love and are bound to Love inextricably. Sin is sinful and has its consequences, and we are beloved, at home in the Perfect Love who is one and three, tender and strong, beginning and end. And because of the mystery of Love, until heaven is there and then, I'm thankful it is here and now.

Spiritual Practice: Breath Prayer

Breath prayer is an ancient form of praying that invites us to "pray without ceasing" as we pray with the rhythm of our breath. The original breath prayer, also called the Jesus Prayer, invites you to pray "Lord Jesus Christ" as you inhale, and "Have mercy on me a sinner" as you exhale. In that pattern, a name for God that is particularly meaningful or needed is prayed as you inhale, with a request being named on the exhale.

Breath prayer lends itself to embracing the both/and because of its natural rhythm: breathing in/breathing out. We cannot survive without doing both. We must find a balance between the two to live. It might sound like this:

> *On the inhale*, Spirit of Truth . . . *and on the exhale*, remind me of *all* that's true.
> Wise Mother, teach me to be tender *and* strong.
> Loving Father, help me to embrace mystery.
> The One Who Sees, help me to see the both/and.
> Mighty God, give me strength to hold seemingly opposite things about [you, me, my spouse, this situation].

Instruction

1. Allow yourself to center down by inhaling and exhaling deeply.
2. Listen for what name for God you feel particularly drawn to.
3. Consider what request you have for God or something you'd like to say to God.
4. Pray the prayer several times, following the rhythm of your breathing. Then remain in silence for a few minutes.

A Few Adaptations

Consider reversing the practice by sitting in silence and letting the Spirit pray through you. Ask God to reveal *your* name and God's longing for *you*. This can be a meaningful experience. You may well hear something like, "Beloved, you are enough," or "Child, wait and rest."

You can also use breath prayer with scripture.

On the inhale: *It is good that you should take hold of the one*
On the exhale: *without letting go of the other.*

On the inhale: *Be still and know*
On the exhale: *that I am God*

Or with a truth you want to take in

On the inhale: *Heaven is here and now*
On the exhale: *and there and then.*

On the inhale: *God, you are a both/and,*
On the exhale: *and so am I.*

FIVE

Olly Olly Oxen Free: Community

And it is still true, no matter how old you are, when you go out into the world it is best to hold hands and stick together.
—Robert Fulghum, *All I Ever Really Needed to Know I Learned in Kindergarten*

The reason life works at all is that not everyone in your [circle] is nuts on the same day.
—Anne Lamott, *Plan B*

I grew up in an era when "come home when the streetlights come on" was how my parents navigated curfew when we were kids. Living in northern Kentucky, it didn't get dark until late on summer evenings, so it left plenty of time for playing with friends in the neighborhood. Sometimes I would find myself in trouble with that much unsupervised time (like when my friend's older sister taught me how to smoke when I was eight), but more often it led to fun times of listening to my neighbor, Roy, play his banjo on his porch stoop or playing a round of hide-and-seek with neighborhood friends. Those summer nights hold sweet memories.

"Olly olly oxen free," was the cry to indicate it was safe to head in if you hadn't been found. I remember the mix of emotions I felt if no one discovered my hiding spot—glad to have chosen such a concealed place, a little afraid I'd been forgotten, and thankful to be back with the others when the call sounded to come in. Robert Fulghum references the iconic childhood game and how it often mirrors our complex relationship with wanting to isolate yet wanting to be known, especially in times of difficulty and heartache. "Hide-and-seek, grown-up style," he says. "Wanting to hide. Needing to be sought. Confused about being found. 'I don't want anyone to know.' 'What would people think?' 'I don't want to bother anyone.'"[1]

When difficulty comes our way, we often have such a mixed response to community. We can long to be surrounded and cared for, while simultaneously wanting to isolate with our grief, anger, or fear. We may have never experienced such intense afflictive emotions, and it can feel vulnerable to be seen and known in such a raw place. Hiding may feel like the best option, yet somewhere in us we long to be sought.

Certainly, we can be hurt by our community rather than supported. Sometimes we stick a toe in to "try out the water," only to discover that the person we've entrusted with our story isn't safe, as they start giving us unsolicited advice or quoting scripture rather than holding space for our pain. As our story unfolded, I had some friends I never heard from again once the news broke. One came alongside us for a season and then decided he couldn't come any further. It was painful, for sure. And yet what I'm learning over the years is that that was more about their limits (and we all have our limits) than about our story being too much. It may have been too much for some—but that's not the equivalent of it being too much in general. I shared with a few others who didn't hold what I offered in confidence, and it created more for me to deal with than I had capacity for at the time. I know many who sense that being truly honest about what's going on in their lives will frighten friends, family members, or employers and potentially lead to even more negative circumstances like getting fired or being shunned. They may accurately assess that those in their current community don't have the capacity to handle the truth of what's happening. Sadly, that often sends people further underground and into isolation.

When a loved one dies, we can be buoyed by the support of those around us, thankful for meals brought and the kind words spoken about the one who has passed. On the flip side, I've known of those in mourning who often felt angered by the well-meaning, yet unhelpful things said to them. "God needed another angel." "There's a reason for everything." These are rarely helpful sentiments but things we grasp for when we don't know what else to say. A friend of mine was tossed into the deep end when his nine-year old daughter was diagnosed with a rare form of cancer. While he and his wife were largely grateful for the love and support their family received, he also had multiple experiences that led him to post on social media "Things not to say to someone whose child is sick."

One of the things that people would often say to me in the early years of our story was something like "You're so strong. I could never do what you've done." Ugh. I didn't want to be in a situation that called for me to "be so strong." At times I actually felt like screaming, "Please quit telling me I'm strong!" And truthfully, none of us knows what he or she would do in a given situation until we're there. Another comment I received was "This is one of the worst things I've heard. I can't imagine" (maybe even followed up with "And you're being so strong"). Again—not helpful. I think people were trying to be supportive to validate my pain and the gravity of the situation, but it often landed like a punch in the gut instead.

So, yes, community can be messy. We are hurt in relationship—and, thankfully, we are also *healed* in it. I couldn't find a support group for other spouses dealing with infidelity, so a friend and I started one. We found five others in similar situations, got a workbook with solid curriculum, and gathered every Thursday night for about a year. We came together to be a witness to one another's pain, to say to each other "That sounds difficult," "You're not alone," or "We see and hear you in your heartache." During that season, one woman in the group lost both of her parents within six weeks. We could do absolutely nothing to change that reality on top of the marital chaos she was navigating, but we could be present to hold space for her while she grieved. Somehow it lessens our pain a little when we are seen and heard in it.

When we experience loss, no matter how great or seemingly small, community is an essential component of how we heal. We need safe places to speak our pain aloud, whether it's about being passed over for a promotion, missing a child that's gone to college, or mourning a friend who committed suicide. While most often our wounds can't be "fixed," we are able to move forward in our grief when others around us witness our pain. While our loss is deeply personal, and truly no one knows what our specific loss feels like, it is when we are seen and known in our pain that it begins to shift. Sometimes community travels with us as we experience a full sense of resurrection from our grief. Sometimes losses are so deep that we must simply make space in our soul for them, and our community helps us to soften into a sorrowful acceptance of our reality.

And while each loss is personal and some are even very private, grief and loss connect us to community. We have all known loss. Each of us has experienced pain. If we allow it, our losses can link us to one another, a shared sense that this world can be challenging *and* beautiful as we seek to endure together. No one else was in my shoes as my story unfolded—and yet because of community around me, I wasn't by myself. I was "alone together" with others. It made all the difference.

Over the last several years, I've given much thought to the types of community that are most helpful in the face of heartache. Twelve-step groups or support groups focused around experiences like grief, divorce, or betrayal are often a cool drink of water to someone experiencing a drought-like condition due to the lack of a safe community. I've met hundreds of people over the years who feel the freedom to show up and be more authentic in these types of groups than they can be with people they've known most of their lives. People who are "in recovery" from things like alcohol or sex addiction, a painful divorce, betrayal, or a deep depression tend to be more honest because pretenses aren't accessible any longer. And while each person's story can be honored for its uniqueness, we find comfort in knowing that others have experienced similar things. We come away thinking such blessed, hopeful thoughts as *I'm not crazy, Other people have survived this*, and *Maybe there could even be redemptive things for me in this.*

I'm aware that "recovery community" is so appealing because of its authenticity. By and large, people show up with what's really going on. The exposure to this kind of community can be an on-ramp to learning how to have meaningful community in our lives no matter what we may be facing. It gives us the vision that belonging and being seen and known are what we're wired for.

Psychologist and theologian Dan Allender is known to say often that we can't "see our own face" and, consequently, need others to see us and speak truth in love about what they see. We need community if we are going to be well.

———————

During my three years in seminary, I experienced a depth of community that, in love, truly helped me see myself. The six men and women in my cohort were spread out in various ministries across Chicago with different supervisors for our practicum. We would often use our time in our weekly small group to process what we were learning/questioning/experiencing about ministry, leadership, God, and ourselves. One day, right before our gathering, I had a run-in with a colleague. Something I had done had triggered her, and she confronted me about it while standing in my cubicle. Lots of other employees were around, and I was all too aware that her disapproval with me was being heard by everyone in that area. I held it together briefly and then headed to meet my cohort for lunch. One of the guys took one look at me and said, "What is *wrong?*" I came undone and just wept.

Never before had a coworker been so disgruntled with me or my work. My group was supportive, loving, and kind. They were angry on my behalf and held space for my emotions. While I think we all knew I was overly impacted by it, they gave me space to look at why I was so stirred up when I was ready. As my group filed out, Sheryl and I were the only ones in the room. I'm convinced that because we were learning in our group to say to one another "What do you see in me? What do you observe?"—along with a holy whisper of the Spirit—I felt prompted to ask her, "Do you think I'm overreacting?" Without missing a beat, she put her hand on my knee, looked me in the eye with love and compassion, and said, "Yes. And are you ready to go on a journey to figure out why?" Not the response I was expecting. And absolutely the response I needed.

That day I couldn't see my own face. I needed community, in truth and love, to tell me what they saw—both my pain in the moment and an awareness that it had deeper roots (which so much of our pain often does). The whole experience proved to be a watershed moment. I began to do the work to peel back the layers of seeing that I'd built my self-worth and identity with flimsy building materials of image management, people pleasing, being known as the "responsible one," and approval addiction. Without community, I would have likely only nursed my wounded pride with defense mechanisms of eating or blaming (not that I still don't do some of that. It took a long time to walk into those woods. It takes a while to walk out).

The thing about pain and suffering is that it will shine a light into the crevices of how things are going on the journey of becoming our true selves. Without disruption and upset, I think I would have settled for continuing to wear "other people's faces."[2] But on that day my community helped me begin to find my own.

I love the definition of *Olly olly oxen free*: "A catchphrase used in children's games such as hide and seek . . . to indicate that players who are hiding can come out into the open without losing the game."[3] Healthy community invites us to come out into the open in ways that are safe and supportive. No one loses. As I have observed over the years, transformative community will reflect a few fundamental truths. While not an exhaustive or sequential list, the following stand out:

We learn to be a gracious host for ourselves.

The second greatest commandment, according to Jesus, is that we love others as we love ourselves. How we love ourselves is so important that Jesus declared it the template for how we love others. When we are learning to be gracious hosts, we become gentle observers rather than harsh critics. We speak to ourselves in the way we speak to our friends. Just stop and think about that for a moment. If we regularly said things to our friends like "You're such a screw up!" "How could you have missed that?" "What were you thinking?!" "You are so stupid!" or "You look really fat," then we probably wouldn't have many friends. "The soul speaks its truth only under quiet, inviting, and trustworthy conditions," writes Parker Palmer.[4] We must learn to be safe and gracious hosts for ourselves if we really want to hear what our souls have to say. When I encounter someone who is harsh and critical, I don't want to spend much time in their presence. I instinctually want to create some distance. I wonder if that same principle applies to how we relate to ourselves. When we create a harsh internal environment, we want to create distance. Maybe that's one of the reasons we end up not learning how to be present with ourselves.

Once I was driving a group of friends to dinner, and, more focused on the conversation than the driving, I got turned around and had to make a U-turn to get us headed back in the right direction. We were meeting some others, and my mistake was going to make us a little late. One of the women in the car commented that I was far calmer about it than she would have been. "I would be beating myself up if I were the one driving, saying some really critical things to myself. You seem really calm . . . *are you actually calm*? And if so—how is your inner critic not on overload? Tell me how to do that!"

"Lots of therapy," I said, laughing. But it was true. By then I had been doing layers of work to shed the lie that my value is found in being perfect or not upsetting someone else. It seems like a small thing, but sometimes it's those seemingly unimportant incidents that prove to be windows into our souls. Later that night I recalled an experience years earlier when I had been in a similar situation, only this time one of the passengers in the car was silently fuming at me for getting us lost and making our group late. (In hindsight, I think his shame got triggered for being tardy and it came out as blame toward me.) I basically had a shame attack of my own as I drove and, in my emotional chaos, got us even further lost. The juxtaposition of the two experiences gave me a picture that, thankfully, I was learning to be a more gracious host to myself despite the fact I may always be directionally challenged.

We create inviting and trustworthy conditions by being gracious hosts for others.

One of the redeeming benefits of going through really painful things is the realization that often you don't need someone to say something profound; you just need them to show up. Sometimes it's even most helpful when they say nothing other than, "Wow. This is tough. I don't know what to say." As followers of Immanuel, God with Us, we seek to love others by *being with* them. Often, that largely involves listening well. We don't "should" on others by telling them what they "should" do to fix their situation, nor do we "at least" them: "At least he didn't suffer" or "At least you're young and can try again to have another baby." We don't preach or give advice, and if we truly believe we have a good observation, we ask, "Do you want feedback?" And then we honor how they respond. Once I asked one of my young adult sons if he wanted my observation about something, and he said quickly, "No. Not about this." Trust me, I was ready with something brilliant and insightful, but I had to honor his request and say nothing. He needed me to be gracious and present, but that day he didn't need my words.

Part of creating trustworthy conditions for others is that we learn to ask them what they need rather than trying to determine that for them. So many of us struggle naming our needs. Most of us didn't grow up getting asked "What do you need?" or learning to ask that of ourselves. Some grew up with a parent who was such a force that the rest of the family orbited around them like the planet around the sun. That kind of environment (whether intentional or not) sets up children to believe only one person in a family could have needs, and it was everyone else's job to meet them for that other person. Part of being a gracious host is befriending our loved ones by asking, "What do you need?" It doesn't mean we can always meet the needs, but it communicates two important things: It's good and even necessary for us to be needful, and they are the best ones to determine their needs for themselves.

At the end of each year, I invite my group members to do a year-end review, looking back over the previous twelve months. The day they share their reviews is one of my favorites all year, as I hear how they've seen themselves grow and change or take honest ownership of work they need to tend to.

Without fail, one of the more common awarenesses is the gift of learning to listen well because of being in community. One of my group members, Sandy, recently had a meaningful experience when her eight-year-old granddaughter spent the night. As Sandy was saying goodnight, her granddaughter, Emma, began to cry. Sandy pulled up a chair next to Emma's bed and asked, "Can you tell me a little about what's going on?" Through lots of tears, Emma began to pour out lots of jumbled emotions. A new baby had joined her family, and Emma was feeling really left out and alone. Sandy knew that Emma's parents (Sandy's daughter and son-in-law) were seeking to have some time with just Emma. She also knew they were working hard to provide for two children and were often tired. Sandy said her old instinct was to talk Emma out of her feelings, something like: "You're not alone—your parents love you!" "Didn't the three of you just go to breakfast the other day after they dropped the baby off?" Or worse: "Aren't you grateful for your baby brother?" Instead of saying any of those things, Sandy listened. She validated Emma's feelings. She didn't try and talk her out of them.

"I can assure you," Sandy told us, "I didn't use to listen like that. In fact, maybe what I did before wasn't really listening but hustling someone back into a place that was safer for me. I'm learning how to make room for someone to be where they really are." What a difference it makes in our families, our primary communities, when we are safe listeners. "Our listening creates sanctuary for the homeless parts within the other person," writes Rachel Naomi Remen.[5] That day, Emma's fear around the transitioning landscape in her family and what that meant for her connection to her parents found a "home" in her grandmother. It was no longer homeless.

Sometimes part of being a gracious host is paying attention to what gets stirred up in us when we're in community. When someone says something we disagree with or have a strong reaction to, we can do as Parker Palmer suggests and practice wonder rather than judgment. "I wonder why she feels that way?" "I wonder why I'm having such a strong reaction?" "What's that about for me that I kind of want to punch him right now rather than keep listening?" Or "Why do I want to crack a joke and lighten the mood rather than sit with this friend who is hurting?" Self-awareness and ownership will always lead to safer community. The absence of either tends to create communal chaos.

As I moved through my own grief, I found that the most gracious hosts were those who had been willing to do the work of moving toward their own pain. For some in my life, that meant they had experienced a similar story. For others, the loss was of a different sort, but either way it didn't take me long to know who was comfortable with grief and sadness and who wasn't. People who move toward their own pain—rather than medicate it, deny it, or minimize it—learn to embody empathy. Because they are willing to feel their pain, they have developed emotional muscles to sit with others in theirs. They don't need to fix the pain; they can simply be with someone in it.

My dad used to tell the story of John Claypool, pastor for a season at Crescent Hill Baptist Church in Louisville, Kentucky, where he and Mom attended when Dad was in seminary. Around that time, John's eight-year-old daughter, Laura, was diagnosed with leukemia and tragically died three years later. John courageously allowed his congregation an inside view of his grief as he and his family traversed that journey. A few years later, one of John's friends had a similar experience when his child died at a young age. The story is told that John called his friend one day, not long after the child died. "I won't say much," John said. "Only this. The bottom *holds*." In the face of anguish, we often wonder if, in fact, the bottom will drop out. But fellow strugglers on the journey who remind us it won't are actually part of the reason it doesn't.

I also had a few friends who hadn't yet developed the capacity to embrace their own pain (whatever its source) but were self-aware enough to know the difference. "I'm not really the one to talk with you about this," a friend said. "I don't really do that. But I'll come help with laundry." Another shared, "I know this hard thing happened. It makes me too uncomfortable to talk about stuff like this, but I want you to know I love you." I really appreciated their self-awareness—as well as their love and tangible support. Far more detrimental are those who don't realize they haven't moved toward their pain and try to hustle us into a place that's more comfortable for them.

While being a gracious host is largely focused on another person, the wise host will allow another's suffering to impact him or her. There's quite a difference between seeing someone as the identified patient whose life is a mess while yours is in good shape versus coming alongside as a companion on the journey. Sometimes we want to keep our distance because we don't want to look at our own stuff. Other times, the pain is so deep it stirs fear that we could face such pain ourselves. If we allow it, part of the beauty of community is that "bearing one another's burdens" is a reciprocal flow for everyone involved. I've had four friends tragically lose children far too early. At times, I wanted to keep my distance because of the vulnerability of it all. A few years after her daughter died, my friend, Laurie, shared with me that she was learning to surrender to the truth that death is a part of life—and that if God allows death, God must also provide us the capacity to navigate it. That changed me. Not just her words, but the fact that I've watched her walk that out.

We recognize that community is far more than a good idea; it's actually our design.

"Then God said, 'Let us make humankind in our image, according to our likeness'" (Gen. 1:26). Scripture tells us that God the Eternal Parent, Son, and Spirit worked together to create humankind, male and female alike, in the image of the Trinity. The Trinity is the original community, relational at its core, and we are designed in that likeness. Just as God, Son, and Spirit are one and yet three, we are individuals and yet somehow not whole without others. We are communal beings. Community isn't just a really good idea; it's our wiring, our very essence. We need it to be whole, to be well. It is also true that not knowing who we are apart from others sets us up to be overly dependent on them for our sense of worth. We must nurture our own individual beings. Yet if we are not ultimately rooted in a safe community that we return to, we won't live into the fullness of how we were created.

In the fifteenth century, Russian painter Andrei Rublev created an icon of the Trinity. Now referred to as "Rublev's Icon," the painting is a beautiful depiction of the three angels that visited Abraham (see Genesis 18:1-8) and symbolizes the Trinity. The figures are seated in a circular position. Each has a rod that signifies equality among the members, and each wears a shade of blue to indicate divinity. The figure on the far left is the Parent, and the one in the middle is Jesus. The Parent and Son are gazing lovingly at one another. The figure on the far right, the Holy Spirit, is gazing down and gesturing toward a small rectangular object that historians believe was originally a mirror. The implication is powerful: As we gaze at the Trinity, we see ourselves invited into the circle. We are included. Our place of belonging is at the table with God the Loving Parent, Son, and Spirit.

We are made in the image of the relational, communal Trinity. This is how we are called to live out our days. The pain I've experienced throughout my life, over and over, has drawn me toward community. Certainly, I've resisted this and have even isolated myself at times. Yet, on my better days, I know I'm not intended to be alone. By design, I am communal. And the only way for me to be whole is in community.

A few years ago, Greg and I longed to be in a community where members could be present with one another in ways we had experienced in some of our recovery groups. So we started our own small group. It was designed to be a place where we could show up and ask one another: "How are you . . . *really*?" It wasn't started as a recovery group per se. And yet, in the time that our group has been together, we've collectively experienced a great deal of loss we've had to recover from: infertility, job loss, miscarriage, addiction, marital separation, a brush with cancer, marital difficulty, and the diagnosis of a child with Lyme disease and depression. Several members in our community have been diving into some old painful family-of-origin wounds. Four of us have lost parents. Two of us have moms with Alzheimer's. We celebrate too: babies being born, businesses being started, new jobs, moves, kids graduating, group members reaching important milestones like graduating from grad school or seminary, and many of us embracing a faith that feels more authentic as we set aside old constructs that don't. We talk about things we're discovering as we keep doing our own work or share stuck places where we're struggling. When chaos or pain makes it easy to forget, we remind each other of what's true: *You are loved. God is bigger than this* (whatever the "this" happens to be in the season).

I'm grateful that one of the redemptive benefits of our story is a core belief that authentic community is beautiful and necessary. It can be tempting to believe otherwise when I struggle to be vulnerable or I fear being rejected. "We have to find our way back to one another or fear wins," says Brené Brown.[6] Rather than allowing my fear to keep me from leaning in and showing up, my pain has shown me that I can't go it alone. A beautiful understanding of the Trinity as the original community tells me I was never intended to.

We "stay at the table" when things get messy.

Parker Palmer's essay "On Staying at the Table: A Spirituality of Community," addresses the truth that—as essential as it is—we will be disillusioned by our community. Someone responds to us hurtfully, a friend pulls away, or a family member doesn't show up for us in the ways we need during a painful season. We are tempted to get up from the table and leave or distance ourselves from the relationship rather than engaging and working through the difficulty. Sometimes, because things get toxic or unsafe, the best of difficult choices may be to leave. When that isn't the case, though, there is an invitation for formation if we'll lean in. "In the spiritual life," Palmer writes, "disillusionment is a good thing: it means losing our illusions about ourselves and each other. As those illusions fall away, we will be able to see reality and truth more clearly. And the truth is that we can rely on God to make community among us even—and especially—when our own efforts fail."[7]

Thankfully, as we grow into emotionally and spiritually mature adults, we find our way to trusting God more. We surrender to the truth that we will be disheartened with community at times—and God is present among us to bring healing, growth, and more accurate perspectives about others, ourselves, and God. Ironically, it allows us to be less guarded and more available to others. "The community we have yearned for is among us," Parker Palmer writes, "in exactly the measure that we are able to discern God's presence in our midst."[8]

May it be so. May the pain of our loss sharpen our vision to see that we are called to live out the truth that we are communal beings, experiencing God's presence among us, in us, and through us as we engage with one another. May we stay at the table with the Trinity—which allows us to stay at the table with ourselves and others. And may we celebrate that we are made in the image of Community—and therefore are hardwired for connection.

Spiritual Practices: *Visio Divina* and Covenant Groups

Visio Divina—*visio divina* is Latin for *sacred* or *divine seeing* that draws on the principles of the practice of *lectio divina* (divine reading). *Visio divina* is slow, thoughtful contemplation that invites you to pray with your eyes as you meditate on art.

A. On the Internet, locate a picture of Rublev's Icon. Allow yourself to enter into a time of prayer, asking God to speak to you through this image.

B. Open your eyes and take in the painting. Allow your eyes to focus on the part of the painting you notice first. Gaze on that section of the painting for a few minutes. Then close your eyes, holding that part of the image in your mind's eye.

C. Open your eyes again and take in the whole painting. Notice if a word, emotion, or desire is stirred in your heart. What thoughts or questions does the image create in you? What do you feel? What holy whispers and/or invitation do you hear from God? Observe the painting for another few minutes and then close your eyes briefly in prayerful rest.

D. Open your eyes and take in the painting, this time responding to God. How do you want to respond to the movement you feel or the invitation you sense? Continue to gaze upon the image as you rest in prayer, then close your eyes briefly.

E. As you close this time of prayer, take in the image a final time. Soak in the beauty of art and the comfort of God's presence as you reflect on this experience.

Covenant Groups—a covenant group is an intentional, authentic group of people who decide to live out community with one another. The group is specifically designed to help and encourage one another and to be seen and known.

The practices include the following:

- Sharing your authentic stories with one another
- Letting others know you well enough to speak the truth in love to you
- Regularly gathering together to remind each other of the truth that we are beloved
- Finding healthy practices that shape and form us into the image of Christ
- Focusing more on being with one another and sharing authentically rather than study
- Living out the "one anothers" of scripture, such as love one another, confess to one another, be kind to one another, forgive one another, bear one another's burdens, teach one another, belong to one another, and be devoted to one another
- Intentionally planning fun experiences together (game nights, parades with the kids, picnics)

Consider whom you could ask to join you in a covenant group. Start with a set time (six months to a year) and then reevaluate at the end of that time frame. For more detailed information about covenant groups, see Adele Ahlberg Calhoun, *Spiritual Disciplines Handbook: Practices That Transform Us*, rev. ed. (Downers Grove, IL: IVP Books, 2015).

SIX

Clean Anger

Anger . . . exists for a reason and always deserves our respect and attention.
　　　　　　　　—Harriet Lerner, *The Dance of Anger*

There is a sense of being in anger. A reality and presence. An awareness of worth. It is a lovely surging.
　　　　　　　　—Toni Morrison, *The Bluest Eye*

I n the first few weeks after our marriage exploded, I sat in the office of my potential therapist. At one point as I was pouring out my unfiltered story, I stopped and apologized. "Sorry. My language has gotten really salty," I said. "I hope that doesn't offend you."

Without missing a beat, she leaned forward and said, "Isn't f* a beautiful word? Sometimes it's truly the only one that fits. But it's like a fine spice," she mused. "Use just enough, and it seasons the dish. Use too much, and it ruins the whole thing." With those words, I knew two things immediately. I loved this woman—and I had found my therapist.

In the midst of such profound loss, I was faced with a level of anger I had never before experienced. Initially I felt more shock and grief than anything, but the anger would bubble up and spill out in ways that seemed chaotic and outside of my control—and sometimes with very colorful language. It would also lurk in dark corners in my soul, weighing me down because I simply didn't know what to do with it or how to express it. While I had often heard Paul's words to the Ephesians to "Be angry, but do not sin," what I took from that was a far greater emphasis on the second half. It was almost as if the command at the beginning was said in a muffled voice with a hand over the mouth—while the second part was shouted clearly: BUT DON'T SIN WHILE YOU'RE DOING IT. I didn't want to "sin in my anger," but I sure didn't know how to "be angry" in ways that were clean and sacred.

One Sunday afternoon while we were separated, I tried to reach Greg. I vividly remember calling and calling, only to get his voicemail. I needed to confirm the schedule for the kids for the upcoming week, and the longer he didn't pick up, the angrier I got. Finally, by the time he called me back, I was seething. "Where have you been?" I said through gritted teeth.

"I was in church," he said quietly. "The place down the street from where I'm living holds services in the afternoon. I'm sorry I missed your calls." While I couldn't admit it to him in that moment, something within me knew I was having a $100 reaction to a $20 issue. I was starting to realize I had to find a way to deal with the anger that was churning deep within and needed a healthy outlet. My anger that afternoon had far less to do with his not answering his phone and far more to do with the pain of betrayal and the humiliation that had come with how public our story had become. I had to get in there and wrestle with the other $80.

I had journaled about my anger, which was helpful but only to a point. I tried reading to Greg a list of all of the things I was angry about—and it sounded more like an observant reporter than a spouse in anguish. Even though I knew in my head that I had so many valid reasons to be angry, I couldn't quite articulate it from my soul. I now see that it actually takes great courage and vulnerability to get clear about anger, to come out from behind the "safe" wall of inexpression and voice clearly and plainly what we are angry about. Whether or not I had an unnamed core belief that "good people" or "good Christians" don't get *that* angry, something in me got held up when I'd try to access my anger. I've heard it said that typically we fall into two camps: We either lean toward sadness that is masking anger, or we more easily access anger that is veiling sadness. It was becoming clear to me that I was the former. Somehow in my heart and mind, "sadness" was more acceptable.

A few days later, I called Sheryl and asked if she'd meet me at the local thrift shop. We bought a box of old dishes and headed to a vacant grocery store. Armed with my purchase and a permanent marker, we located a good spot behind the abandoned building and settled in. Sheryl would hand me a plate, and I would write on it a word or two that embodied something I was angry about. Then I'd hurl the plate at the brick wall and watch as it shattered, the fragments of the plate covering the ground. We didn't talk. She was my silent witness as anger, sadness, and grief churned in me. I wanted to yell and scream, but for that afternoon yelling and screaming weren't quite accessible. What did happen, though, is that it got the logjam loosened, and the anger started to rumble. I'm fairly sure that back alley of the Piggly Wiggly had never been such holy ground.

A few days later, I called Greg, who was just leaving his support group (and answered his phone quickly this time). "Would you be willing to meet me?" I asked.

"Yes, he said. I'm glad to. Can you tell me what it's about?" I think he heard in my voice that he needed to prepare for what was ahead.

"I'm mad as hell," I replied. "And I want you to hear it."

To his credit, he replied, "I'm on my way."

We met in a parking lot, and I got into his car. For the next two hours, I poured out my anger as I held him accountable for the ways he had hurt me and our family. By no means was it pretty—but something in me knew it was healthy (or at least healthy-ish). Greg received my anger. He heard it and was present with me in it. It was actually one of the first times I had hope that maybe we could survive the chaos we were in. He would tell me later that he had the same thought. Ironically, it was probably the most intimate and connected thing we had experienced together in the few months since we had been separated.

It's important to note that, for a host of reasons, not everyone can "receive" another's anger. Maybe the one who is angry isn't actually "clean" in his or her delivery, so it doesn't feel safe for the one receiving it (in other words—it's rage-filled, sarcastic, pouty, blame-y, or self-righteous in nature). Another possibility is that the one listening has some painful wounds around how anger was experienced in his or her home growing up. Just hearing a more intense inflection in another's voice or seeing angry facial expressions is too triggering. It can often take time and practice to trust that anger can truly be healthy.

And that's the thing about *clean* anger. It creates intimacy with others, with ourselves, and with God. When one of my sons was a teenager, he would isolate when he was angry with me (or just angry about something). Once when I sensed him pulling away, I asked if he would be willing to just name it—to look me in the face and tell me why he was angry. While it wasn't easy for either of us, he courageously made eye contact and began to talk. The energy in the room and the dynamic between us shifted. In the context of our relationship, he was able to find his voice and be heard. I remember observing as his face and body turned toward me. We were more connected after that exchange, not less. It was a powerful awareness for me of how *relational* the healthy expression of anger could be. And interestingly, that experience grounded me in the truth that if I could hear and even *welcome* my son's anger (however imperfectly)—how much more would God welcome me to turn toward God and do the same? It led me to wonder, *What if healthy anger has been God's idea all along?*

Anger often gets bad press because it's often experienced in such skewed ways. It's either stuffed down and then leaks out sideways as snark, sarcasm, indirect jabs, blame, or shutting someone out for days (or years). When unexpressed outwardly, it can seep inward, leading to depression, bitterness, and contempt. Sometimes a person ineffectively expresses anger so that, rather than voicing it clearly, it comes across as nagging or trying to control another to change. And of course, it can come spewing out as rage. Leslie, a client of mine, refers to her rage as a "come-apart," that horrible experience of allowing your wiser self to be hijacked by your shadow side and discharging your messy anger onto those around you.

What if we were to embrace the truth that *clean* anger is necessary and holy? God designed us with that emotion, and we have the capacity to feel it in healthy ways. What if it actually "deserves our respect and attention?"

Psychologist and theologian James Finely says this:

> Anger is the God-given emotion that restores the boundary that was broken. There is no healing without anger. Anger isn't rage or resentment. Nor is it whining. Whining is anger coming out of a very small opening. To find your anger is to say, "I will no longer passively go along with this that doesn't value me." If you forgive before you get angry—you'll repress it and it will leak out. And if you don't find healthy ways to express it—you'll sit on a loaded coil of anger that will explode, making you become almost like the one who hurt you in the first place.[1]

On paper it makes sense that anger is necessary for healing. But for many facing loss, anger seems out of reach and, as I certainly discovered, is often convoluted with our early family and/or faith "rules" (written or unwritten) about anger. I know of a woman who lost her young son to cancer and was talking to a friend of mine who had just lost her daughter in a car accident. The first woman was trying to comfort and encourage my friend for the road ahead, describing many of her emotions. Right at the end of the conversation she added, "And thankfully I haven't gotten angry. I've been able to avoid it." Those words stayed with my friend, landing in a place of deep knowing that something about that seemed off. I would guess that the woman felt like she was following the "rules" that it wasn't good to allow herself to get angry or, more accurately, to express her anger. And I would wonder if, in fact, she was angry, but it was either leaking out or seeping in as depression.

What if part of the healing process is simply *to get really mad*? To rail against the cancer that took your son. To verbalize with safe friends your fury at the drunk driver who plowed into your dad. To be angry at the mom who refused chemo early on. To voice to church leaders your anger at how they treated a member of your community. To scream at Mother Nature for a tornado that wiped out your home. To curse the perfect storm that led to your husband's death. Ah . . . yes . . . *Anger exists for a reason and deserves our respect and attention.* So what does clean anger look like?

- *It's owning it for yourself.* It sounds like "I am feeling angry" rather than "You made me so angry." It looks like apologizing to your kids when you have an $80 reaction to a $20 thing they did (and then getting in there and wrestling with the other $60).
- *It's kind.* Even if it's direct, the words aren't full of contempt, attacking someone's character.
- *It's clear.* It's being willing to have a "strong and separate self," as Harriet Lerner calls it, to come out from behind any sense of being "frustrated" or convoluted in our wording. It's being really vulnerable to honestly say, "I'm feeling angry."
- *It doesn't have another agenda.* Rather than trying to wield anger to get someone to change their behavior, you are finding your voice to simply name what's true for you.
- *It really is about the anger.* To the best of our awareness, we are striving not to use anger to shield us from the vulnerability of feeling our grief. Sometimes we discover that profound sadness is underneath the anger, and if that happens, we allow the anger to lead the way to feeling our grief rather than hiding out in our anger.
- *It's responsible.* If first I need to word vomit and vent some things that really *aren't* kind—I'll do that work separately to offload chaotic, angry energy. Maybe that involves throwing plates or a modified version of that, like throwing eggs. Two women I know had a great deal to be angry about and decided to head into a wooded area one day armed with several dozen eggs. They held space for each other as each took her turn, writing on eggs and then sending them one by one crashing into tree trunks and splattering over rocks. Some find hitting a punching bag or running until they can't go another step therapeutic. One client told me he weeded his garden with a hoe, naming aloud something specific he was angry about as he struck each weed. Another shared with me that she pray-screamed her anger at God into her pillow (while simultaneously asking for help). Sometimes the anger is such a visceral part of us that we need to give it an avenue to drain out of us without doing harm.

Clean anger also involves **doing our work around all of the layers of the anger**. "If we're hysterical, it's historical," so the saying goes. To be "clean" in our anger is to explore the history underneath its intensity. Kiera, one of my support group members, was understandably and rightfully angry at her husband for his deception and unfaithfulness. For a season, he walked out and left her and their children and chose his addiction to an affair partner and pornography instead. As he hit bottom and began to walk a road of recovery, it was clear he was committed to being well. Over the years, he regularly owned how hurtful his actions had been and sought to repair the relationship by seeking to live his amends. Kiera wanted to stay in the marriage but struggled to see her husband as anything other than one who had been unfaithful. Three, even four years later, she would sometimes still refer to him as "the betrayer." And while, yes, that was true (he had betrayed her), something about her demeanor felt like it was more about her than him. One day she was processing this in group and asked us to ask questions or offer her challenges about this stuck place in her (such a courageous thing to do).

"Say more about the anger," someone said. "How old is it?"

"When was the first time you were betrayed?" another group member asked.

We watched as she closed her eyes and tears rolled down her cheeks. She sat quietly for a while, and then responded with her eyes still closed, watching with her internal eye as old memories bubbled up and came to the forefront of her mind. "I was twelve years old when my dad divorced my mom and left us for another woman. They married quickly and he became a stepfather to her children who were similar to the ages of my siblings and me. One night he came to a junior high basketball game in which he sat in the stands with his new wife to watch his stepson play. I was a cheerleader, but he merely waved at me as he left with his new family. My mom wasn't going out in public much, so she wasn't in the stands. She was so hurt and enraged by the divorce that I didn't dare tell her what had happened. And I felt so humiliated, I didn't talk to anyone."

There, buried long ago underneath the pain of her husband's infidelity, was the betrayal of the first man in her life. It's not that her dad's choices were the only source of her anger; clearly, she had valid reasons to be angry at both men. Yet without doing the deeper dive, she was holding her husband responsible for *all* of her anger when some of it pre-dated him by a few decades. Over the next several months, Kiera began to tease out what belonged to her husband, and what she needed to hold her dad accountable for. The logjam started moving, and she was able to start releasing her anger at her husband and to find the courage to start looking at the pain from her dad.

———————

So back to salty language. Interestingly, scientists have been fascinated about swearing because most everyone does it. For years the think-ing was that cursing would only make a situation worse because it was an expression of a person's helplessness in the face of pain. But more recently, researchers have proven that swearing helps people increase pain tolerance, providing space to endure the anguish.[2] Some circum-stances simply call for more than "Geez" or "This stinks." We have to be careful with it. To be sure, swearing can be detrimental and harm-ful. When directed at someone, especially children, swearing and name-calling is anything but clean anger. In fact, the research also indicated "If they want to use this pain-lessening effect to their advantage they need to do less casual swearing."[3] (Apparently the researcher himself doesn't swear!) The encouragement here is small doses for healthy rea-sons. Like my therapist said . . . a little seasons the dish, and a lot ruins the whole thing.

Maybe swearing really isn't your thing. I only ever heard my dad swear once in his life, and it was in reference to that "damn fundamental-ism." It was indicative of the anguish he felt from watching his beloved denomination being overrun by legalism. When she couldn't get the door unlocked or the gas pump engaged, my mom might swear then quickly downshift into giggling. I think she cracked herself up when she was venturing out on the edge. It really wasn't their thing—or at least they didn't feel they had permission for it.

Maybe it's become your thing, and you didn't know you knew such words, yet you're finding it healing. I call that *transformational swearing*—that language that gets at the depth of our pain and allows us to describe our anguish with words that are sizeable enough to represent it. In safe spaces and with safe people (not *at* people), it's giving voice to our anger that says: *This is not okay. Nothing about this is okay.* Researcher Brené Brown has spent her career sitting across from people as they tell her about some of the most painful and difficult moments of their lives. "After fifteen years of this work, I can confidently say that stories of pain and courage almost always include two things: *praying and cussing.* Sometimes at the exact same time."[4]

By now you might be thinking, *What about such scriptural teachings as Ephesians 4:29, "Let no evil talk come out of your mouths, but only what is useful for building up, as there is need, so that your words may give grace to those who hear"? Doesn't that apply here?*

The word translated *evil* (or *unwholesome,* as other translations such as the NIV use) comes from the Greek word *sapros,* which can also be translated as "rotten" or "worthless." It's wise for us to enlarge our understanding of what that may encompass. A person may never swear but regularly engage in "worthless" speech that is purposefully inflammatory or critical of another. I've been in the church long enough to hear gossip disguised in the form of a prayer request, with a "Bless her heart" added on the end for good measure. When cursing is used to tear another down or is intended to be hurtful, it is rotten, *without value.* However, when a person is seeking to move through grief and loss, transformational swearing is that visceral language that captures the depth of pain. It's what we yell in the privacy of our car, it's what we scribble and underline five times in a journal, it's what we say aloud as a friend holds us while we sob or as we throw plates at a wall. Rage and anger may need an avenue to find their way out of our core being. To that end, transformational swearing is *worthy* indeed.

———————————

Years ago, I attended a retreat that focused on emotional and spiritual health. Following the weekend, we gathered one evening the following week to share with our loved ones ways the weekend had impacted us.

Many of us testified of doing another lap of forgiveness, learning to love ourselves better, or having an experience that helped us embrace the courage to take a risky next step. One of the women on the retreat was in her 80s. For a while, she had been doing her work around the intense pain she had known as a child. Part of what she had lost was her capacity to feel and express clean anger. As you can imagine, anyone in their 80s doing that kind of work was adored and respected by those of us who were younger. When it was her turn to share, she walked to the front of the room with dignity and grace—and began to cuss like a sailor. She simply streamed curse word after curse word. I had a direct view of the director of the counseling center, who at first was stunned and then moved into a profound, joyful knowing that what was happening was sacred. With safe people and in safe ways, we were her container, holding space for her as she vented what had needed to be said for years. It was nothing but holy.

I know this may be a stretch for some. Glennon Doyle says it well: "If you are someone who considers cursing to be a weakness, please bear with us cursers with great patience, and daily forgive us. If you are someone who considers intolerance for cursing a weakness, please bear with us with great patience and daily forgive us. Persevere. Try to see through to the God in us."[5] In the letter to the Romans, Paul says it this way: "Those who eat must not despise those who abstain, and those who abstain must not pass judgment on those who eat; for God has welcomed them" (14:3).

There's a print by artist and spiritual director Melanie Weidner hanging in my office that I adore. It reads "Damn. I mean thank you. Yes, thank you."[6] Sometimes there's a lot to say "damn" about. The goal of anger isn't to stay there but to help heal the boundary that was broken and find our way forward. Because eventually, if we do our work, we find our way to gratitude. And it is not a false sense of gratitude that wants to avoid facing into our pain but rather a thankfulness that comes from recognizing the beauty and necessity of this God-given emotion of anger and the freedom and serenity it brings when we find clean ways to express it.

In her beautiful book of blessings *The Cure for Sorrow*, Jan Richardson offers this prayer:

> Trust
> that the other face
> of anger
> is courage,
> that it holds the key
> to your secret strength,
> that the fire it offers
> will light your way.[7]

Thank you. Yes, thank you.

Spiritual Practice: The Sacred Discipline of Plate Throwing

Giving our anger avenues to be expressed "cleanly" is a significant way to follow the command to "Be angry but do not sin" (Eph. 4:26). Consider inviting a safe friend to either join you or be a silent witness as you give a visceral expression to your anger by throwing plates or eggs.

1. Gather old plates from a thrift store or get a few dozen eggs and a permanent marker.
2. Identify a safe place you could throw plates or eggs.
3. Enter into a posture of prayer. Ask God to direct your thoughts and give you freedom to be cleanly angry, free from judgment toward yourself and without malice toward another. As you think of something you're angry about, write it on the plate or the egg. It can be a word or phrase that is meaningful for you. Then smash it against the surface. Ask your friend to hand you another when you're ready. Throw until you can't think of anything else to write.
4. These are the God-given fruits of this practice:

- Learning to offload anger in healthy ways so that it does not leak out on those around you or seep into your heart in the form of contempt, bitterness, or resentment
- Validating the need to say, "What happened to me was not okay because it violated my humanity"
- Learning to move through anger so you can release into the peace of surrender
- Engaging the forgiveness process by allowing yourself to hold someone accountable for his or her actions through feeling your anger

SEVEN

Take Off That Ugly Sweater: A Look at Shame

We can face shame as an invitation to look into the eyes of the One who does not condemn."
—Dan Allender and Tremper Longman III,
The Cry of the Soul

A few months into our journey, I was having breakfast with a friend. She was involved at the church where things had unfolded and knew much of the story. As challenging as it was, I had chosen to stay on staff for several reasons—the fact that I was the primary breadwinner being chief among them. Working in a place where our story was so public was kaleidoscopically chaotic. At times it would be redemptive and healing to be with those who were kind and supportive; but turn the dial and the view could rearrange completely into something painful and paralyzing. The turmoil of it weighed on me that morning at breakfast. As I unloaded how I felt and shared various conversations I'd had in the church hallways, my friend sat back in the booth and looked at me. "Girl—you've got to take off that ugly sweater," she said kindly. "You're all wrapped up in shame. It's time to take it off."

God bless people who tell you the truth in love.

That awareness hadn't yet crossed my view through the kaleido-scope. I was overwhelmed by so many different emotions that kept me from seeing that I was cloaked in shame: shame for what had happened, shame for how public it had been, shame for what I hadn't seen, shame for some of the responses of others. She was right, and I would need to learn how to shed my shame.

While there are many afflictive emotions that we want to sidestep, two of the difficult emotions we want to avoid the most are grief (as men-tioned earlier) and shame. The fact that you're reading this book is an indication that you're likely dealing with grief—and shame is universal, so welcome to the party.

You may be thinking, *I don't think I have shame* or *That's not really my issue.* While we certainly can be at varying levels of learning to practice shame resilience, I believe, this side of heaven, we will all have shame to some degree. It's like saying, "I don't ever feel [anxious, sad, ambivalent, frustrated]." Shame is an emotion we feel. It can also shift into becoming a toxic core belief.

It's at this point that a brief definition would be helpful. Interest-ingly, that is not as easy as it would seem. In *The Soul of Shame*, Curt Thompson says, "even defining [shame] is no easy task, which . . . is part of shame's intention. For its elusiveness is a key element of its power."[1] I have often experienced shame like a thick fog that rolls in, keeping me from seeing clearly, or a toxic gas that creeps under the door. It may be elusive and hard to grab on to, yet its message is undeniable: I am bad or flawed.

Brené Brown has given us her working definition that "shame is that warm feeling that washes over us, making us feel small, flawed, and never good enough."[2] Thompson would add that it's also the sense of being powerless to change our circumstance. In other words, "I do not have what it takes to tolerate this moment or circumstance."[3]

Given that the two feelings we often want to avoid most are grief and shame, it's especially chaotic when the two show up together. For a variety of reasons, we may feel shame about our grief. Maybe we believe we should be "over" something by now and feel shame that our grieving process continues. We notice others' reactions that communicate they think we should be further along (or at least that's how we interpret it), and so we start to curtail being honest about how we're really doing. Another common scenario is that we ourselves are uncomfortable with or weary of our grief, so we shame ourselves into being "done" with it by telling ourselves, *Other people have it worse. You should be grateful for what you do have.* Yes, some losses are more intense, but it shifts into shame when we "should" on ourselves to shut down the necessary flow of healthy grieving.

Think about our knee-jerk reaction to crying in public. "I'm sorry" is often the first thing we say as we shed tears in front of others. We fear we are making things awkward, so we apologize, either because we are ashamed of our grief or because we are aware of our vulnerability in it. We can feel shame about our grief—or we can even "grief shame" others. "Grief shame happens when we rush someone to heal before they are ready" or "when we judge a person's expression of grief."[4]

The reasons we might be triggered into shame around grief and loss are many:

- We feel shame for something we've done or left undone.
- We feel shame because of not seeing something that we wished we'd understood earlier.
- We feel shame for not having made the most of the time we had with someone before they died.
- We feel shame for hurting another.
- We feel shame for not being able to say goodbye.
- We feel shame for not doing more.
- We are particularly prone as parents to feel shame for something that happened to a child (such as an illness, an accident, bullying, a divorce, depression) because we are hardwired to believe we can protect them.
- We feel shame for not advocating enough for ourselves.
- We feel shame for believing we made a poor choice—one that in hindsight seems like it was so obvious to choose differently than we did.
- We feel shame that we're still grieving.

- We feel shame for not grieving as much as we think we should.
- We feel shame for losing patience with a sick or dying loved one.
- We feel shame for feeling relief when a sick loved one dies.
- We feel shame for the shape our marriage or family is in.
- We feel shame that we survived.
- We feel shame that we stayed.
- We feel shame that we left.
- We feel unable to affect change to a painful situation—maybe because we truly can't change the reality—but it lands in us in a place of shame because we are powerless. While it may be subtle, it's often present.
- And sometimes we feel shame about our shame. Shame squared.

As mentioned earlier, shame is both an emotion and something that can shift into a crippling core belief. John Bradshaw, one of the first researchers of shame, explains, "toxic shame, the shame that binds you, is experienced as the all-pervasive sense that I am flawed and defective as a human being."[5] The vulnerability of loss seems to leave us more susceptible to this toxic kind of shame; like fog, it can seep its way into our dark night, making it that much more difficult to see our way clear, especially when we are already hurting.

I felt shame after my dad died because the intense grief following his death far outweighed what I'd told myself it would look like in the months leading up to his passing. Because I had navigated deep painful waters in my marriage, I found comfort in believing that I'd been through profound loss and therefore had some "grief muscles" that would help me through this. Some denial was probably woven in there too. I was facing losing my dad to death and my mom to Alzheimer's almost simultaneously, and the vulnerability of those catastrophic losses was overwhelming. The "home base" I had known with my two loving parents was careening off a cliff without any guardrails. After Dad died, a sense of shame welled up in me, a critical inner voice that said, *You underestimated your grief. What were you thinking? Of course you'd hurt this much.* And sometimes, just for kicks, the shame voice would toss in a bonus for free: *And by the way—are you sure you did everything you could have done for him?*

Maybe there was another treatment, another doctor, another protocol we could have followed. Shame is a tremendously good second-guesser.

As referenced in another chapter, I wasn't a very "gracious host" to myself at times in my grief, and unchecked shame was often responsible for that. In hindsight, I actually think there was wisdom in how I tried to prepare myself. It was the opposite of saying "You don't have what it takes to face this," and instead, I was seeking to coach myself that I would be able to navigate it. But because what unfolded was grief of a different sort and the loss was so intense, the critical voice of my shame won over. In my pain, I wanted something or someone to blame, so I blamed myself for thinking I could handle the pain (as if that was going to help). Shame may not be logical, but it's certainly determined.

———————

Bart Sumner and his family experienced the unthinkable when his ten-year-old son, David, died of a sudden traumatic brain injury while playing football. In explaining what happened, Sumner writes: "He was fully suited up, wearing the most advanced head protection available today, he had never had any head injury prior to the incidence, and he had been coached properly and was not doing anything that invited such a tragedy." Then, about that description he says:

> That sentence, with all its qualifications of what was not done wrong and how there was no one to blame or point fingers at is where the shame lies. . . . I have come to terms with the fact that David's accident was just that, a horrible accident. I logically know, and have accepted, the fact that there was no one to blame and nothing that was done that brought about his death. But even though I know this and have forgiven myself for letting him ever play football in the first place, the shame lingers. If it didn't, I wouldn't need to make those qualifications every time someone asks me what happened.[6]

Anyone, especially a parent, can read this loving father's words and sense the anguish and the heartache. One of the ways shame rears its head in grief is when we find ourselves again and again qualifying what happened. We want to overexplain because we're hoping it will eventually quiet our own chaos and bring relief. Or we intuit that we would have critical thoughts if we were hearing the story. Sumner is spot on. It's where the shame lies.

If we're honest, we've all probably voiced (or at the very least thought) similar critical statements when we have witnessed something painful happening to someone else. We shame them with our inner dialogue (or sometimes with our actual comments), which equates to blaming another. *How could you have missed this? Didn't you see what was happening? You had to know. Were your smoke detector batteries up to date? Why in the world would you allow your child to go to that party?* And/or we have a running commentary of self-righteous thoughts: *I would never let my child play football. I would leave if my spouse ever did that to me. She should have nagged him to get to the doctor sooner. Maybe something could have been done. I make sure my husband gets his physical.*

Our self-righteousness often indicates that we are afraid, fearful that something so painful and chaotic could happen to us. And out of that fear, we use shame to distance ourselves from that level of vulnerability. Whether we are grieving or witnessing another in pain, shame is always lurking nearby, promising to knock us out of truth.

It's not pleasant looking at our shame, and it's even more unnerving to consider what it could teach us. And yet, if this is an arena where we lean on God as midwife, then maybe God is lovingly using our current situation to bring to light the hold that shame has on us.

And here's the thing: While our current situation may be exposing our shame patterns, those patterns almost always have a much older history than our present-day pain. If we've come out of a shame-based culture (such as our family of origin or our church community), we'll bring shame to whatever we're faced with, and often the more pain we're in, the more intrusive the shame voices will be. Worth noting is that "shame-based culture" may run the gamut from a fundamentalist upbringing full of black-and-white thinking to far more subtle expressions of shame, such as how our parents or teachers responded to us when we made poor choices or missed the mark in sports or school.

We can also have experienced shame when we needed our parents to move toward us and they were distant, so we made a meaning of their distance, believing we aren't lovable or that something is wrong with us. Similarly, an ethos of shame can have been created by witnessing critical exchanges between our parents or by hearing our caregivers speak negatively about our bodies or their own. Thompson's enhanced definition of shame that includes the idea that "I don't have what it takes to tolerate this moment or circumstance" shines great light on the many nuances of shame. Shame is a shapeshifter, and part of what we learn as wise adults is how to spot it in its various forms.

Brené Brown coined the phrase "shame resilience": the hopeful truth that we can learn to shed our shame and develop strength in love and compassion to address it when we find ourselves pulled into its vortex.[7] To develop our shame resilience, it helps to understand the various ways we respond when shame shows up. While we may react differently to shame each time it appears, it tends to be some variation of the following three ways:

- When we believe the lie that we aren't enough, we start placating those around us to gain approval or affirmation. Maybe that comes in the form of flattering another or staying quiet about what we really think or need. We can also placate by saying things like, "I'm such a screw up." When we communicate with someone we've hurt while we are in the midst of our own shame storm, it creates real chaos. The one hearing that may struggle to agree because it doesn't seem healthy to respond with "Yes . . . you're such a screw-up"; yet, they also aren't sure how to advocate for themselves in the face of someone who is hunched over in shame. Shame often takes up so much room that there is then very little space for someone else's feelings.
- Another common response to shame is that we pull away and hide. In a distorted train of thought, we convince ourselves that isolating is the "safest" option. Ironically, it often creates an even richer environment for shame to fester, because we don't have anyone to help us check our lies and find our way to the truth.

In that place of hiding, we say things to ourselves like, "If people only knew what was really going on" or "I'm such a fraud."

- Yet another reaction to shame is to get angry and power up. That often comes across as blame, finding fault in someone else and wanting to transfer the angst we feel onto another. We can also direct the blame back to ourselves. We are powering up against ourselves when we turn that critical voice inward and say things like: *How could you be so stupid?? What in the world were you thinking? You should have known better.* It is a safe bet that shame (in the form of blame) is involved whenever we are "shoulding" on ourselves or someone else.

The good news is that these reactions are not our only options. When seeking to live as wise adults, we can shed the shame by finding our way back to truth. In fact, if we're in shame, we know we're believing a lie (at least one!). One of the ways we come out from behind shame is by asking what lie(s) we are believing. For example, am I believing something like "There is something fundamentally wrong with me," "I'm bad," "I'm damaged goods," "I'm not enough," or "I don't have what it takes to face this situation"?

Another aspect of shame resilience is learning to reach out to community. Shame hates to be spoken aloud. I'm thankful for safe friends that I can call and who call me and say: "I am in a swirl. Can you talk?" When we courageously step into the vulnerability of being seen and known in our shame—and others receive what we share with empathy and compassion—shame begins to loosen its grip on us. Layer by layer, we begin to shed it.

I feel so grateful when a group member says something like "I'm having a shame storm around how I reacted to my neighbor/friend/spouse/child/colleague, and I want to talk about it." Some might even add, "Actually, the last thing I want to do is talk about it, but I'm learning it helps to lessen this chaos, so here goes." And sometimes, when we are in shame and don't yet realize it (like me that morning at breakfast), our loving community can kindly encourage us to start exploring the lies we're believing.

Another important piece of finding our way back to truth is teasing out the various emotions that may be swirling. Gaining clarity around them and their differences is part of how we find our way back to solid ground. As we defined earlier, *shame* is that feeling that tells us that we are bad, flawed, not enough, or don't have what it takes to face a situation. *Guilt* is the experience of feeling bad about a choice to do something or leave something undone. It's the feeling that washes over us when we believe we've made a mistake. *Embarrassment* is feeling foolish in front of others. When we're embarrassed, we'll often say to our safe people, "You're not going to believe what I did," and we're likely to eventually laugh about what happened. *Humiliation* is the emotion we feel when our status is lowered in front of others.

Years ago, I attended my nephew's early Saturday-morning basketball game. Not long after I entered the gymnasium with my travel mug, the game stopped. The referee motioned to the coaches to huddle up—and then pointed way up in the bleachers to where I was sitting with my family. With the crowd looking on and the players confused, the referee proceeded to play some dramatic version of charades, communicating to me: *You need to exit the gym pronto with that travel mug!* (You can just picture the hand motions.) Despite the fact that I'd sat through many morning games at my kids' school with a drink, that wasn't allowed in this gym (and clearly I must have missed signage that told me otherwise) and the ref wanted to be sure I knew it. One of the keys to knowing we're humiliated is that we're angry, believing the intense response we received wasn't necessary. By that definition, I can assure you I felt humiliation that morning.

You may be asking what the value is in understanding these various emotions that are similar to shame. Unless we begin to understand ourselves and our emotions better, we just lump all our distressing emotions together as "negative" emotions to avoid. As a result, we often miss exploring what they can teach us. (*Why did that experience trigger a shame storm in me? Why do I feel guilt over what I said to my friend?*) Emotions themselves aren't positive or negative, good or bad. Some are more enjoyable than others, but all our emotions tell us something about ourselves and how we're responding to a situation. In fact, one of the patterns that our loss may have exposed is that we want to avoid all types of "afflictive" emotions, a guaranteed recipe for living emotionally stunted lives.

When we are grounded in the truth, we can own that we hurt one another, and part of being emotionally and spiritually healthy is the capacity to acknowledge when we've wounded someone we care about or made choices that don't line up with our values. While shame may be our first involuntary response, it doesn't have to be the place we stay.

Conviction is a Christian term for the feeling and experience of living outside of a loving God's desire for us. As people of faith, we seek to attune to what God wants for us. Conviction is that nudge from the Spirit, inviting us back into healthy living when we've made choices that don't honor God, others, or ourselves. We are most sensitive to conviction when we are making room to be quiet with God and with ourselves, and when we are in community with others who are doing the same.

Godly sorrow is often linked to conviction. When we feel sorrow and remorse, they allow us to look another in the eye and say, "I'm so sorry for the pain my actions have caused." It's based on ownership. Shame ("I'm such an awful person") isn't our only option. In fact, a person's capacity to vulnerably communicate remorse and sorrow while making eye contact, instead of showing head-down or eyes-closed shame, is such a good indication of healthy growth.

In her writing for those grieving a miscarriage who discover how shame can intertwine itself with anguish, Kelly Gerkin suggests, "part of healing is to shed the weight of a cloak that isn't meant to fit."[8] It sounds a lot like what my friend said to me when she implored me to take off the ugly sweater. I was never intended to be wrapped up like that, which is why it had me in such a bind. We weren't designed to live cloaked in shame. But when shame shifts into something more than a passing emotion, we start hunching down from the weight of it. Because our eyes are figuratively (or in some cases literally) looking downward, we can't see ourselves clearly, much less a healthy path forward.

In the story of Jesus' raising Lazarus from the dead, we find an important detail right at the end of the story. "The dead man came out, his hands and feet wrapped with strips of linen, and a cloth around his face. Jesus said to them, 'Take off the grave clothes and let him go'" (John 11:44, NIV). For that new season of Lazarus's life, those grave clothes were not intended to fit. A resurrection had occurred, and the strips of linen meant for death were no longer needed. Notice whom Jesus commanded. Jesus told *them*, the friends and community, to let Lazarus loose. So often we don't realize what we're "wearing," or we simply don't have the capacity to take off our own grave clothes or ugly sweaters of shame. We need kindness, empathy, and truth spoken in love from our community to help us see when we're cloaked in shame and to help us find our way out of the bind.

Throughout the Gospels, we see Jesus repeat that pattern with his words and especially his actions. With women and men who were likely to be in a shame storm, imagine how Jesus might have invited them to name the lies their pain was leading them to believe and take off garments that weren't intended to fit.

To the woman who had been bleeding for twelve years: "Daughter, your faith has made you well; go in peace" (Mark 5:34). *You are important enough for me to stop and notice as I make my way to a sick little girl. Don't believe that your illness counts you out or makes you damaged goods. I'm glad you touched me. Take off that ugly sweater.*

To Zacchaeus: "I'm coming to spend time with you in your home. You, too, are a son of Abraham" (see Luke 19:1-10). *Don't believe the lie that your poor choices or your physical stature make you unlovable. Take off that ugly sweater.*

To the woman caught in adultery: Jesus called out the truth of those wanting to stone her and trap him: "I do not condemn you. Leave your life of sin" (see John 8:11). *No one is blameless, including those men who wanted to stone you. Your life is worth saving, and you have the chance to make* *other choices. Your worth is not found in what you can offer someone sexually. Take off that ugly sweater.*

To the woman crippled for eighteen years: Jesus called her forward in the synagogue—out from where women had to be separated from men—touching her, healing her on a sabbath: "Woman: You are set free from your infirmity. You, too, are a daughter of Abraham" (see Luke 13:10-17). *You and your healing are more important than the law, so much so that I'm willing to break it on your behalf. Don't believe the lie that you don't matter or that your body or your womanhood is something to be ashamed of. Take off that ugly sweater.*

To the one born blind and his parents: Jesus said, "Neither this man nor his parents sinned" (John 9:3). *Shed the shame others have been trying to put on you because they have tried to assess you through the lens of an either/or theology. You are beloved and blessed. Nothing, especially your physical handicap, changes that. Take off that ugly sweater.*

To Peter: "Do you love me? Then feed my sheep" (see John 21:15-19). *I forgive your betrayal. And your choice to deny me doesn't invalidate your capacity to lead. Take off that ugly sweater.*

Jesus calls us out of the lies of shame and into the freedom of truth over and over again. In its final words, John's Gospel tells us "there were many other things that Jesus did; if every one of them were written down, I suppose that the world itself could not contain the books that would be written" (21:25).

I can't help but wonder if, in every encounter Jesus had, he was helping expose the lies people believed that kept them cloaked in shame. Jesus (then and now) invites humanity to shed the lies of shame and step into truth. Out of shame, into freedom, over and over again, so much so that if every encounter were written, the world itself couldn't hold that many books.

Let's help one another take off those ugly sweaters.

Spiritual Practice: Centering Prayer

Centering Prayer is a way to open ourselves to God beyond words and thoughts. It is not an attempt to replace other forms of prayer but rather is a practice that moves beyond conversation with God to silent communion with God. Thomas Keating, one of the major proponents of Centering Prayer, said that it is "not an end in itself, but its deep rest loosens up the emotional weeds of a lifetime."[9] Shame is so often one of those "emotional weeds." Instead of acquiring something in this practice, Centering Prayer encourages the falling away of those things (like shame) that keep our true self hidden.

The guidelines for Centering Prayer are as follows:

1. Choose a sacred word to represent your desire to consent to God's presence and action (such as Abba, God, Love, Jesus, Trust).
2. Choose a comfortably seated position and close your eyes. Allow yourself to center down and silently introduce the sacred word as your intention to consent to God's movement.
3. When you engage your thoughts, body sensations, images, or feelings, return ever-so-gently to your sacred word.
4. After your time of prayer, stay in silence with your eyes closed for a few minutes.

The recommendation is to aim for two periods of twenty minutes daily, once in the morning and once in the evening. Give yourself space to work up to that length of time. You may want to start with ten or fifteen minutes.

For more information, see Martin Laird, *Into the Silent Land: A Guide to the Christian Practice of Contemplation* (New York: Oxford University Press, 2006).

EIGHT

It's a Marathon, Not a Sprint: Forgiveness as a Process

Let us say
the wound will not be
our final home—
that through it runs a road,
a way we would not
have chosen
but on which we will finally see
forgiveness,
so long practiced,
coming toward us,
shining with the joy
so well deserved.
　　　—Jan Richardson, "The Hardest Blessing" (excerpt)

One day, in the early days of our crash and burn, I talked over my situation with a friend. She listened for a while and then interjected, "You know . . . you're going to have to forgive Greg." It had been three weeks since our world had blown up. I stammered through a response and tried to find my words. "Yes," I agreed.

"But this will take some time. It will do more damage than good if I rush through forgiveness. This is going to take a while."

I still remember where we were sitting when we had that conversation. I felt angry at first—and then in hindsight I understood she was working from a framework I was all too familiar with, one I had even believed and taught others. I didn't really know what forgiveness would look like going forward. I only knew that the construct I had for it up to that point (forgive quickly and move on) wasn't going to hold.

In almost every story of loss and heartache, a need for forgiveness is woven into the narrative, often with complex layers. We need to forgive someone for how they've hurt us or forgive ourselves for creating anguish for someone else. Maybe we need to show mercy to our bodies for letting us down or forgive God for how we perceive God has not shown up for us. Sometimes we need to forgive an institution such as a church or a denomination or something as intangible as Mother Nature.

Since I didn't know what healthy forgiveness could look like, I had to explore what it wasn't. While this isn't an exhaustive list, the following are key components.

Forgiveness is not saying that what happened is okay. So many of us get hung up believing that forgiving is somehow equivalent to saying, "It's okay that you did this." Nothing makes hurtful actions okay, and our forgiveness doesn't change reality. "Grace cannot change the moral order," writes Jerry Sittser. "What is bad will always be bad."[1] Yet we can learn to live in the tension of seemingly opposite things: what happened can be egregious *and* we can forgive it. We can't change what happened. We can have a say in how it will affect who we become.

I began to recognize that I had to hold Greg accountable for what he had done and how his infidelity and dishonesty hurt me and many others in the process. A first step in forgiving had to be naming the detriment of the actions and allowing myself to feel the anger. At times I wanted to see something different, but I couldn't stay grounded in reality without facing the truth of what had occurred.

Forgiveness is not the same as reconciliation. We must forgive if there is to be reconciliation, but reconciliation may not always be possible. Forgiveness is something that I need to engage for the health of my spirit and relationship with God and is not dependent upon the other person. Reconciliation, however, is different. If the person that wounded me is owning his or her actions and working to put things in place so the offending behavior will not happen again, then that creates safety and helps to rebuild trust—which can potentially lead to the relationship being reconciled. But if a person is not demonstrating changed behavior, it may be necessary to set healthy boundaries and not reconcile the relationship in the way it was experienced previously.

A woman I know named Maria lived on the receiving end of her dad's rage all through her childhood and into her adult years. Not long after her mother died at the young age of sixty, Maria's father came for a visit. He got triggered one night during a discussion about where to go to dinner and turned his rage (which, of course, wasn't about a restaurant selection) onto Maria. Before the incident was over, he had backed her into a wall while spewing obscenities in her face. Somewhere in the combination of her grief over losing her mom and her weariness of her dad's rage, Maria found her "holy hell no." She asked her dad to pack up and leave, and with tender strength, drew a boundary that he couldn't return until he had gotten some counseling around his unhealthy anger (that she had come to understand through her own healing wasn't about her and had never been). Sadly, he chose not to seek any help, which meant it wasn't safe for Maria to reconcile the relationship in the way it had been lived out before. Maria found ways to love him from a distance, seeing him in groups with other family members. His unwillingness to make any changes, however, made it unsafe to fully reconcile.

This doesn't mean that we give up on reconciling. We watch and wait for when it may be safe to do so. Maybe there are changes down the road. And even if there aren't, we are still able to make wise and loving choices toward the other.

Forgiveness is not contingent on someone apologizing. Sometimes we may need to forgive someone who will never apologize for their behavior or someone who is no longer living. In the situation mentioned above, Maria walked out a process over time of forgiving her dad for the many times he had raged at her and the myriad ways that had affected her—not because he owned it and apologized but because she wanted to do the work to free herself from the burden she carried. While it may prove much more difficult, we can forgive someone even if they don't take responsibility for their behavior and apologize; it's spiritually and emotionally healthy for us to do so—and to believe that we are held captive to wait for them to ask forgiveness doesn't acknowledge that we have the power to "change the things we can." We may also need serenity to accept that, if there is no ownership or change in behavior, the relationship may be one that is released, not reconciled. It's quite possible a lap of grief will be needed for us to lament what was never made right by the one who harmed us. And we are still capable of choosing freedom. Such a both/and!

Maybe we need to forgive a group or an organization so big we aren't sure who we would even converse with—and no one is contacting us to offer an apology. Again, reconciliation may not be possible, but forgiveness is still our choice. In *The Dance of the Dissident Daughter*, Sue Monk Kidd writes about her need to forgive an entire denomination for their degrading stance toward women and the pain that had caused her and so many. After running that marathon for a season, she made the choice one Sunday morning to find her way to the church of her youth. While the service carried on inside, she simply laid a bouquet of flowers on the front steps, symbolic of the forgiveness she had come to offer. While her relationship with the denomination couldn't be reconciled, a peace within her unfolded as she released the pain it had caused her.[2]

Forgiveness is not the same as trust. While both trust and forgiveness are needed in rebuilding a relationship, one does not equate to the other. Forgiveness is that process I engage with myself and God as I seek to let go of the hurt done to me. Where trust has been broken, it will be rebuilt over time. Wise adults offer trust where trust is earned, but not carte blanche and especially not with someone who has deeply wounded us. This is not the same thing as being cynical or stingy with our trust. Rather than offering "positional trust" because of a position someone is in, we offer trust where trust is earned by actions that demonstrate trustworthiness. This is true for a spouse, pastor, elder, doctor, friends, or family.

Forgiveness is most certainly not weak. Healthy forgiveness that engages a process requires strength, courage, and vulnerability. Truthfully, it's one of the bravest things we'll ever do, even if we hear a critical voice in our heads telling us we are weak for forgiving. Consider stories you've heard over the years of a mother forgiving her son's killer or a man forgiving a father who abused him. We are moved by the strength and depth of character it takes to forgive. In *The Book of Forgiving*, Desmond Tutu writes about Bishop Malusi Mpumlwana, who was arrested as an anti-apartheid activist and suffered extreme torture from the South African police. In the midst of his torture, he had an astounding insight about his torturers: "These are God's children and they are losing their humanity. We have to help them recover it." Bishop Tutu reflects, "It is a remarkable feat to be able to see past the inhumanity of the behavior and recognize the humanity of the person committing the atrocious acts. This is not weakness. This is heroic strength, the noblest strength of the human spirit."[3]

Forgiveness is not a sprint. My heart aches at the stories I have heard of so many counselors or clergy, pastors in particular, who have told people who have been deeply wounded to forgive without hearing more of the story, validating the pain, or helping the person set healthy limits. When we don't allow others the space for their own process, our anxiety and incapacity to sit in the unknown eclipses what the other person needs. Forgiveness then becomes a box to check rather than a process to walk. Quick forgiveness in the face of significant hurt is often cheap and done out of a "should" voice in one's head or from a pulpit. It might also be what someone chooses as a way to avoid the work of holding healthy boundaries, deciding instead to "have grace" and forgive. But that isn't grace or forgiveness. It's being so dependent on the relationship for our worth or value that we are unable to make healthy decisions grounded in reality.

So what are some helpful ways to understand what forgiveness *is*? Instead of a sprint, I like the idea that forgiveness is a process—a marathon with multiple laps. While there are some hurts we can forgive in the moment, like a quick sprint down the track, the deep wounds will call for a commitment to the *process* of forgiving. You might remember in high school English class the rarely fun topic of verb tense with the categories of past, present, and future. "Present progressive" is one of the subtypes of present verb tense: *I am running, he is eating, she is waking.* In the present, an action is in progress. It is unfolding. In the face of deep pain, it can be helpful to embrace forgiveness in this way: *I am forgiving. I am running this marathon. It is in progress.*

This also helped me as I wrestled with scripture. I knew I wanted to honor God in how I walked this road, yet I didn't quite know how to do that. Scriptures would float up to the surface, such as "Forgive as the Father forgave you" and "Don't let the sun go down on your wrath." Was my gut instinct of needing more time an excuse not to lean into the hard work of forgiving? What would it mean if the sun went down and I was still angry? I couldn't fathom any prayer I could utter before I went to sleep that would so significantly change how I was feeling by morning. The idea of engaging the process in present progressive form proved helpful. If I'm moving away from hard-heartedness toward being on a journey of forgiveness, then I'm in the process. It's *present*. It's important to add that we can't hide behind the idea of "being in process" to drag our feet. A forgiving process is being vulnerably open to how God is regularly inviting us to surrender our hurt. Even if it's slow, we are gaining traction.

This feels so hopeful to me, knowing that no matter what comes my way, I have the choice to engage a process of forgiveness with another or myself. While the process will look different for everyone, these components are important:

- Identifying the hurt. Identify what was lost, naming the reality of the action(s). It's important to discern what the behavior has cost us.
- Telling the story as many times as necessary to safe people who can hear it.
- If possible and safe, having a conversation with the one who hurt us to communicate our hurt and the way the situation has impacted us.
- Having a dialogue to seek to understand. Again, nothing changes the moral order. But it can be helpful to ask for help understanding what happened.
- Surrendering and letting go, again and again. This gives new understanding to what Jesus may have meant by forgiving seventy times seven. As a painful old memory surfaces, we do a lap of forgiveness work around the track, asking God to help us release the hold it has on us. We run another lap when we learn new information about the story that wounded us. Seventy times seven, we remind ourselves this is a marathon, not a sprint.
- When we feel unable to forgive, we sit "while God prays," bringing sacred movement in our wounded soul.

Liminal Space

"Forgiveness is more a process than an event, more a movement within the soul," writes Jerry Sittser.[4] Once we engage that process, we may find ourselves in liminal space. From the Latin root word *limen*, meaning "threshold," liminal spaces are transitional or transformative seasons in our lives. To decide to engage a process of forgiveness is to enter an in-between space: I'm not in *unforgiveness,* nor can I say *I've forgiven.* I'm in between. When I allow myself to be in this place, it's so often where the Spirit stirs significant movement in me. "A liminal space is the time between the 'what was' and the 'next.' It is a place of transition, a season of waiting, and not knowing. Liminal space is where all transformation takes place, if we learn to wait and let it form us."[5]

My old historic paradigm told me that forgiveness was something I needed to do and do quickly. Yet what if the forgiveness process is a transformative space that changes us? If we aren't changed, in fact, by forgiving, it's likely not forgiveness and has originated from a place of self-righteousness where we place ourselves above another. The judgmental voice in our heads (even if we don't voice it aloud) sounds something like *I forgive you, but I would never do this to you.* Yet when we allow God to move and shape our being, forgiveness becomes a place of transformation. Maybe I haven't done this exact thing to someone—but I have the capacity. One of the many things we can learn from the life of Peter is that we can all underestimate our capacity to betray or hurt another.

———————

My process of forgiving Greg has been a painful, sacred, and freeing journey. Greg took full ownership for his actions and showed deep remorse for his choices. He engaged active recovery from his sexual addiction and invested in repair work with me. As we teach at our workshops at Faithful and True, we sought a three-legged–stool approach to recovery: he was doing his work, I was doing mine, and together, we have worked to rebuild our marriage into something much stronger and healthier than we knew before. While it wasn't a linear process, I've experienced forgiveness toward Greg as shifts and movement in my soul. Even though I referred earlier to the idea that forgiveness doesn't require an apology, the path forward is much smoother when someone validates our heartaches and shows remorse for what their choices have cost us. I'm grateful Greg sought to make the path smoother than it could have been because of his ownership and the way he has sought to live his amends.

Because our story happened in the context of the church where Greg and I were both on staff, another piece of our story was having to traverse how the church responded. That path has been more difficult to navigate. I'll never know what it was like to be in the shoes of the leadership of that church when this story broke. I'm confident it was difficult and challenging. I do know that being on the receiving end of how they chose to walk out this situation has been incredibly chaotic. At times they provided for us financially in ways that were gracious and kind. In some regards, there were very understandable consequences for sinful actions. Also true is that at times they responded with judgment, shame, and harsh boundaries that were incongruent with how I understand the gospel. Particularly hurtful for me was the overstepping by one of the elders, two years into our journey, who shamed me for staying in my marriage, questioning how I could respect myself by any other way than leaving. Without any form of reconciliation with the church leaders, this has been a heartache.

I wish I could tell you I forgave this quickly and let it go. I did not. I wish I could tell you I haven't rehashed these things over and over. I can't. (God bless my safe friends and therapist who have listened to me struggle.) I wish I could tell you that as I write this, fifteen years later, I don't feel any pain or grief over how the church responded to Greg and to me. That wouldn't be true.

Hindsight, therapy, and the tender instruction of God's Spirit have given me some different perspectives. As I dug underneath my hurt and anger, I entered into a liminal space.

Could I respect myself and stay? Once I separated this out from the delivery, it was an important question to answer. So many people I have talked with over the years who have been betrayed struggle with this very question. Prior to our crash and burn, I had made a declaration to a friend that I would leave if Greg was ever unfaithful. In retrospect, I see that statement was made from the comfortable, uninformed position of one who wasn't yet in the middle of a storm. None of us knows what we'd do in any given situation. The last several years have taught me a humbler approach as I observe others, and I'm learning to say, "I'm not sure what I'd do" in reference to someone else's story.

I also had to get grounded in my reasons for why I felt I could be healthy and choose to stay. Our story had many complicated layers, and I'm thankful I was willing to look at the complexities and invite wise counselors to speak into them. I read, processed, and explored. I sought to leave no stone unturned. The formational invitation in this process was to learn to trust myself and trust that the Wonderful Counselor would direct my steps as I sought to make healthy decisions, no matter the subject.

I've also had to explore why I cared so much about what that elder thought. As one of the lead elders, she literally and figuratively represented the church to me. I've had deep sorrow regarding how she and the others handled our story. Honestly, it felt like another betrayal. She believed I had forgiven Greg too early and judged me for it. The great irony is that it's taken me a long season to forgive her and the church that she represented. And, as I've walked this out, I've had to acknowledge that the church is made up of humans, and in our humanity, we will hurt others. The church won't be perfect. It isn't Christ. It's designed to be the body of Christ that points us back to divine, perfect love. We know that pain and disappointment will be part of our experience in church—or in any relationship (marriage, friendship, family, or with colleagues) because that's part of being human. We will get hurt—and we will hurt others, as I know I have done. And that doesn't have to be the whole story. "Let us say / the wound will not be / our final home," is the blessing offered to us by Jan Richardson. Forgiveness offers a way forward so that the "the wound," yours and mine, whatever it is, does not have to be our final destination.

Recently our downstairs' neighbor, a devout Jew, slid a note under our door, letting us know that later that week he would be blowing the shofar (or Ram's horn) on Rosh Hashanah, one of the Jewish High Holy Days. Intrigued with the meaning of this ritual, I learned that Rosh Hashanah is the first of the Ten Days of Repentance, and the call of the horn invites its listeners to awake from spiritual slumber, examine their ways, and return to God.

On the afternoon that he blew the horn, we were taken with the sacredness of the sound. It was mournful and captivating. At first I tried to continue with what I was doing as the call permeated up to our apartment, but eventually I paused to take in the jarring, piercing sound.

I wonder how many times I have missed a call to awaken from my spiritual slumber and tried to press on with my own agenda, avoiding reflecting on the need for my own repentance. The liminal, transformational space of forgiveness brings me full circle: I am invited not only to release others but also to explore where I have hurt and wounded people through my words and actions or lack thereof, ways I have mishandled situations, or times I have overreacted. Humility, grace, and truth allow me to examine where I need to ask forgiveness and seek to repair a relationship. I'm prompted to move out of self-righteousness and into gratitude that God forgives my trespasses as I forgive those who have trespassed against me.

The wound, whether it's ours or one we caused, doesn't have to be our final destination.

Can we complete the process? I honestly don't know if forgiveness has an end. Some losses continue to reverberate for years to come. Sometimes it's years down the road before we see how we've been affected or until we learn another piece of the story. In that case, another lap around the track is likely needed. It doesn't mean the earlier forgiveness work wasn't valid. It may just mean that, as pain surfaces, we will be invited to meet it with forgiveness. And sometimes we walk into full freedom of releasing our pain. Thank God.

To choose not to start the process at all is to stay in unforgiveness. We know we are dug in to unforgiveness when we keep playing the story, the conversation, the events over and over in our minds and hearts without any traction. We wallow in those images rather than examining them for the messages they have for us. We stir up our pain but don't offer it a way to release. And the wallowing starts to change us, bringing the unnecessary "second death" of bitterness and contempt mentioned in an earlier chapter. If you are in unforgiveness, so be it. Sometimes it takes acknowledging the truth of that (and our weariness of it) to make any changes. It can be helpful to check in with ourselves to determine if we have vowed (consciously or unconsciously) that we aren't going to engage forgiveness. If so, it's helpful to bring that out into the open and discern how that is affecting who we are and what choices we want to make going forward.

———————

I met Aliyah several years ago. She was a beautiful, feisty young woman who was on a journey of emotional and spiritual health. While she had been angry at her dad for leaving her and her siblings when they were young, what she came to realize was just how much heartache she had over how her mother had turned her against her dad over the years. Her mom would regularly speak negatively of her ex-husband, hide gifts he sent for the kids' birthdays, and purposefully mess up the weekend visitation schedule, all the while blaming Aliyah's father. As a young girl, Aliyah didn't have the capacity to understand what was happening, and what she mistakenly absorbed was a false message that her dad didn't love her. While she was still angry at her dad for leaving them to be largely single-parented by a mom with such rage, she began to realize how she needed to hold her mother accountable for projecting that rage onto her and her siblings. She regularly saw a therapist as she did several laps around the track about her mom.

Although limited, Aliyah still had contact with her mom. Her mom would visit periodically and was seeking to grandparent differently than she had parented. Aliyah's mother never took ownership for her actions when Aliyah was growing up, and Aliyah knew the kind of relationship she was able to have with her mother would be limited. Yet nothing could limit Aliyah from doing her work. She could bless her mother and release herself from the pain she carried as she navigated the journey of forgiveness.

One evening at the beach, Aliyah found herself drawn to the rhythms of the waves. As she stood on the shore, she entered into a prayer of forgiveness and blessing. As a wave rolled in, she named aloud something she needed to forgive: "You made us believe he forgot about us," or "You hid our presents he mailed and convinced us he didn't remember our birthdays." As the wave rolled back out, she prayed a prayer of release and blessing: "I surrender this pain. I bless and release you." Thankfully, graciously, the wound was not her final home.

I am running this marathon. I am releasing. I am forgiving.

Spiritual Practice: *Lectio Divina*

Lectio divina is an ancient spiritual practice of prayerfully meditating on scripture by listening to it from a heart perspective and allowing it to reverberate in you. Rather than approaching the scripture for knowledge (which is a different spiritual practice), the goal here is to soak in it. Latin for "divine reading," the practice has five steps that can be done individually or in a group setting:

1. **Quiet** (*silencio*): First, create space and time to quiet yourself and center down into a place of receiving what God's Word has for you.
2. **Read** (*lectio*): Read the verse or passage through, allowing it to wash over you. Notice if a word or phrase stands out to you. Listen and pause.
3. **Reflect** (*meditatio*): Read the scripture again, this time reflecting if there is an invitation God is extending to you, especially in light of the word or phrase that caught your attention.
4. **Respond** (*oratio*): Read the scripture again, this time entering into conversation with God about the scripture, what is getting stirred up in you, any resistance you may have, or a response you desire to make.
5. **Contemplate** (*contemplatio*): Read the passage again. This final time wait on the movement of the Holy Spirit as you surrender yourself to God.

Leave silence between each of the steps, allowing room for God to speak, move, and invite.

Seek to use no more than a few verses or one story at a time. Given this subject of forgiveness, consider practicing *lectio divina* with the following:

Matthew 5:44: Love your enemies and pray for those who persecute you.

Matthew 6:12: Forgive us our trespasses as we forgive those who trespass against us.

Genesis 50:19-21: The story of Joseph's response to his brothers.
Luke 15:20-24: The story of the younger son returning home to
his loving father.

Additional Resources

Brenner, David G. *Opening to God: Lectio Divina and Life as Prayer.*
Downers Grove, IL: IVP Books, 2010.

Calhoun, Adele Ahlberg. "Lectio Divina." *Spiritual Disciplines Handbook:
Practices That Transform Us.* Downers Grove, IL: IVP Books, 2015.

Hall, Thelma, RC. *Too Deep for Words: Rediscovering Lectio Divina.* New
York: Paulist Press, 1988.

NINE

Welcoming What Is

Everything belongs and everything can be received. We don't have to deny, dismiss, defy, or ignore. What is, is okay. What is, is the great teacher. *I have always seen this as the deep significance of Jesus' refusal of the drugged wine on the cross (Matt. 27:34).*

—Richard Rohr, *Everything Belongs*

This isn't the marriage I thought I'd have," Susan said. "And it's certainly not the marriage I want. Yet, somehow, it's the marriage I'm in."

Soon after her husband's history of infidelity came to light, Susan came to a support group I was leading. Her husband, Sam, had entered into a recovery process that led to clean and faithful living while she had been actively doing her own emotional work. Despite years of engaging in helpful therapy, they both admitted their marriage could still be challenging as they often bumped up against one another, creating ripples of pain and chaos. The years of counseling had provided tools that prevented their dynamic from being toxic, but "deeply satisfying" isn't how either of them would describe their relationship. For a few years in group, Susan processed her disappointment and expressed deep longing that her marriage would be something other than it was. From a wise adult perspective, she named she could have a childish response to the situation: an internal sense of stomping around saying "no, no, no, no, NO. THIS IS NOT WHAT I WANT!"

Knowing she had the freedom to leave *and* the freedom to stay, Susan allowed herself to mentally and emotionally explore divorce. Over the years she had observed that divorce was sometimes the best of difficult options for others, yet intuitively she didn't sense that was the best path for her. She and Sam loved and felt committed to one another—*and* their relationship had its difficulties. One day in group, she shared that she was beginning to sit with a new question. Instead of *why can't my marriage be better,* she was starting to ask, *Am I ready to accept that, if I stay married to Sam, I will be in a marriage that will probably be challenging? Because of who we are and what we bring out in one another, this will likely never be easy. It can be good and hopefully will improve (and we can keep working to that end), but for today, can I accept that this is what is?*

We sat back and took it in, knowing it was a significant shift. Susan had been expending so much energy railing against what wasn't that it had been challenging for her to accept what was. Her outward posture and facial expressions that morning told us she was no longer inwardly stomping around. Holy movement was allowing her to be peacefully congruent in her body, heart, mind, and soul. She wasn't settling or acquiescing. Instead, she was in the process of surrendering. Surrendering to the truth of what is and isn't and thankfully being open to what that truth could teach her about herself, her marriage, and God.

> *We can only see you in what is.*
> *We ask for such perfect seeing—*
> *As it was in the beginning, is now, and ever shall be.*
> *Amen. (So be it.)*[1]

The above prayer by Richard Rohr invites us to name the truth that God is in what is. Right here. Right in the middle of whatever is presently true.

> I am resentful. *We see you in what is.*
> This isn't what I signed up for. *We see you in what is.*
> My daughter and I are estranged. *We see you in what is.*

My dad left when I was young and never really looked back. *We see you in what is.*

My marriage isn't satisfying. *We see you in what is.*

I am unable to get pregnant. *We see you in what is.*

I feel like God didn't protect me. *We see you in what is.*

My body has betrayed me. I've been diagnosed with cancer. *We see you in what is.*

I don't have a category for my son taking his own life. *We see you in what is.*

My mother is so ravaged with dementia she doesn't know me. *We see you in what is.*

My spouse is gone. *We see you in what is.*

This isn't how it's supposed to be. *We see you in what is.*

My anxiety about the state of our world is heavy and intense. *We see you in what is.*

As you read those words, you may have been shaking your head, wondering how this makes any sense. This may feel like cognitive, emotional, and spiritual dissonance. Often we see God in the "good" and feel abandoned by God in the painful and difficult. The invitation to see God in "what is" seems counterintuitive.

Let me be clear that this isn't the same thing as acquiescence, reluctantly accepting something hurtful or unhealthy without voicing dissent. This isn't settling—where we throw our hands up in the air, choosing a victim mentality that we are helpless to affect change in our situation. And this *absolutely* isn't passively accepting abuse by not drawing healthy boundaries. Sometimes the healthiest thing we can do is find a "holy hell no" to step away from something that doesn't honor our dignity.

So, what does it look like to welcome what is? First, "welcoming" in this context is used to indicate being present rather than being in denial. It's saying yes to being grounded in reality and being willing to ask where God is in it. The goal at hand is this: "What first comes to your heart and soul must be a *yes* instead of a *no, trust* instead of *resistance,*" says Richard Rohr. "When you can lead with *yes* and allow yourself to see God in all moments, you'll recognize that nothing is ever wasted.

Trinity is in the business of generating life and light from all situations, even the bad and sinful ones."[2]

It's worth saying that it may take time to see where God is present. Maybe we're open to it. Maybe we're *open to being open.* We get as many "opens" as we need. One of my early memories is of my parents discussing a situation in which a family's house caught fire and the husband sat outside in his lawn chair exclaiming "Praise God!" as he watched it burn. At age five or six, I vividly remember my mom and dad talking about the incongruency of that response—and maybe even the lunacy of it. (Some families talk sports; mine talked theology.) That isn't "welcoming what is." Welcoming often involves noticing and allowing all of the emotions that are present to be expressed, such as fear, anger, sadness, disgust, or being overwhelmed—and then finding our way (however circuitously) to trusting that somehow God can generate life and light even from this.

———

Just a few weeks before Greg was fired, I had been reading David Benner's *Sacred Companions.* In it, he suggests that, as we have the capacity in our grief, we consider moving from railing against heaven as we shake our fists and ask *"Where are you God?"* to softening into a more open posture of asking *"God, where are you?"*[3] The words may be the very same—but the intent is altogether different. As I lay awake into the early hours of the night our lives exploded, the memory of this different kind of asking floated up to my awareness. I saw it as one of the ways God had gone before me, allowing space for me to consider that I could trust God as this chaos was unfolding. I didn't have this language at the time, yet in hindsight I see I was being prompted to "welcome what was," trusting that even this would not be wasted. I kept a journal about many things in those days, with one section reserved specifically for where I was seeing God. I look back now over that sacred list.

- Gift certificates for nights when I was too overwhelmed to cook
- A bag of groceries from Mary with treats like Twinkies that my boys delighted in

- The letters and cards that filled the mailbox for months with words of support and prayer
- The outpouring of love and support from the volunteers in the ministry I led
- Dinner that Tori fixed and brought to us every Tuesday night for about four months. She would even ask for requests from two boys who were simultaneously bewildered at all that was happening in their lives and glad to see her coming with dinner every week.
- The fact that I led a ministry for hurting marriages—full of volunteers that had experienced something similar. If ever there was a non-judgmental group, it was them.

I saw God in the image of one of those volunteers bent over weeping when he heard the news of our pain. I found God in my inner circle of friends who were willing to be on a journey with Greg and me. I watched God in motion as my family came around me and moved toward Greg. After I called to tell them what was unfolding, my parents went to see Greg soon after they arrived in Chicago. When Greg opened the door where he was staying, my dad spoke first: "We love you, Greg. We always have." In their presence, Greg sat and wept for about twenty minutes, unable to say anything at all. It was a holy moment for all three.

Yes, we see you in what is. Yes.

Seeing God in what is often requires a new framework because typically we want to focus solely on what needs fixed and the quickest way to get there. We tend to believe that slowing down long enough to be present with what's true will let the grief, pain, or anger (or any afflictive emotion) pull us under. I'm not suggesting we don't work on solutions. The Serenity Prayer speaks to finding this balance: *God grant me the serenity to accept the things I cannot change, the courage to change the things I can, and the wisdom to know the difference.* Learning to release into a place of surrender and accept that our current condition is our reality will allow us to be present with Presence. Continuing to resist *what is* keeps us focused on the past, pining for the future, or suffering emotional paralysis. None of those allows us to be present.

As you're reading this, you may be wondering if this is really necessary. Let's start with what happens when we don't learn to welcome what is. When I choose to move through difficulty, loss, and pain in a posture of resistance, a vacuum-like force pulls me toward my oldest and dearest defense mechanisms. The list of options is long—I might be bossy, judgmental, critical, blaming toward others or God. I might be prone to having a tantrum (external or internal) or slide into a place of being jaded or cynical. Or I may create a defense around my heart with people-pleasing, denial, minimizing, hustling for my worth, over responsibility, or a host of other unhealthy behaviors. Historic and familiar, all of the above are examples of coping mechanisms I may have needed at a time when I was young and didn't have the option of operating out of a place of emotional adulthood when hard things happened. I like the language of referring to this part of myself as my "survivor." And given some parts of my story growing up, including experiences that happened and the deprivation of some things I needed but didn't receive, I came up with ways to survive. We all do. Thomas Keating refers to them as our "programs for happiness, which can't possibly work."[*] If I remain in a posture of resistance, it's as if I make a vow that I'm not going to "grow up in all ways" (Eph. 4:15), including emotionally. I choose to cling to my old ways of grasping for security, affection, and control. It may be unconscious, but unconscious vows are perhaps the most dangerous of all. I cling to old programs, believing they will be the best way to protect myself in the midst of heartache.

The opposite of clinging is surrender, which is scary and freeing all at once. It's relinquishing into a place of trust rather than hardening our hearts and/or shutting down in resignation. It's openness to feeling our reality rather than denying it. It's consenting to God's presence and action in it. Of course, if we are going to practice surrender, the necessary question is, "To whom am I surrendering?" If your image of God is punitive, distant, harsh, critical, regularly disappointed, judgmental, and/or absent, it makes sense that you wouldn't want to make yourself vulnerable with a god like that. It would be abusive to do so. Theologian J. Keith Miller has been known to say that you may need to fire that god.

To surrender to God is to surrender to the God that scripture tells us is love (1 John 4:8), light (1 John 4:7), merciful (Psalm 103:8), gentle (Psalm 18:35), kind, tolerant, and patient (Romans 2:4). For many, it's easier to imagine *Jesus* as those things, rather than God, yet Jesus tells us "if you have seen me, you have seen God" (John 14:9). In his beautiful book *Sinners in the Hands of a Loving God*, Brian Zahnd addresses the roadblock so many have with God, a belief that they're fine with Jesus but aren't quite sure of what to do with their felt sense that God is angry, withholding, and hasn't protected them. I love his response, "Jesus is the Word of God. Jesus is what God has to say. Jesus is God's ultimate act of self-disclosure."[5] He repeats that theme over and over in the book, I believe, because we need to hear it again and again. *Jesus is what God has to say*—about you, about me, about our pain, about our loss, about racial injustice, about the state of our world. Just as we can have core beliefs about ourselves that aren't true, it's quite possible that we have core beliefs about God that aren't accurate. Ironically, that may be part of what we need to surrender.

———————

Eli, one of my spiritual direction clients, entered into a time of imaginative prayer, asking God, *Where are you?* And *Why do I feel so alone?* As he sat in silence for a while, the image of Jesus in the Temple as a twelve-year-old boy began to bubble up. He saw Mary and Joseph, frustrated, frantic, and unable to find Jesus. He heard Jesus answer, "I've been here all the time. Here in the Temple." Eli was quiet for a while—and then began to cry tears of gratitude. "*I* am the temple," he said softly. "God has not abandoned me. I've been looking for God only in certain places and frustrated and frantic when I couldn't see God in the way I expected."

Learning to welcome "what is" is a sacred act of trust, saying yes to the truth that God is in all of it. May we ask the God of love for such perfect seeing.

Spiritual Practice: Welcoming Prayer

Welcoming prayer is a way to welcome *what is* while saying yes to God in the midst of it. In fact, *welcome* is the sacred word that you return to throughout the practice. It was designed by Mary Mrozowski as a kind and gentle way of dismantling our false self. It is intended as a companion to Centering Prayer and is a way to say yes to God as you move throughout your day. The prayer has three movements.[6]

First, our daily experiences are the canvas on which God wants to do this work in us. As you feel afflictive emotions like anxiety, fear, sadness, anger, and annoyance, *notice, feel,* and *sink into* those emotions. It's counterintuitive, yet the idea is to welcome what is rather than try to avoid, medicate, or deny your current reality. Notice where the emotions land in your body. For example, you might observe stress in your jaw, anxiety in your gut, or anger in your chest. As you do, pray the words, "welcome, welcome." Again, the idea is not to indulge or wallow in the difficult emotions but rather to acknowledge the reality that you are feeling them.

The second movement is to welcome God into whatever you're experiencing. One suggestion is to use the name "Divine Therapist" for God as you do. Again, welcome God's presence and action into whatever is true for you in the moment by praying, "Welcome Divine Therapist, welcome." It can be helpful to place your hand on your core, for example, as you welcome God into the anxiety you feel in your gut.

The third and final movement of this practice is to pray the two letting go phrases:

I let go of my desire to hustle for security, affection, and control.
And I let go of my desire to change this feeling, sensation, or situation.

Welcome.

While those phrases are challenging to pray, keep in mind that we are each letting go of our *false* self's attempts at hustling for security, affection, and control. We are consenting to God's work in us to grow and develop our true, wise self. Welcome.

TEN

Embracing Our Bodies

Good is the flesh that the Word has become.
—Brian Wren, "Good Is the Flesh"

Friends of ours have twin boys who are thick as thieves while being unique in their own right. Ryder is outgoing and up for a party (or a revolution) at any given moment, while Emmett is more reserved and a real fan of some quality downtime. So it was a surprise to his parents that at his uncle's recent wedding, Emmett was the one to get his groove on for hours once the dancing started. He later told his mother that the only thing wrong with the evening was that he didn't get to keep dancing (they left at 11:30 p.m.). Uninhibited, Emmett comes fully alive on the dance floor.

On a different occasion, I watched one evening in church as a three-year-old girl danced to the music while we sang. She made twirling into an art, entirely present in her own world. It was beauty unfolding. I have no memory at all of what we sang, but I readily recall thanking God for creating us with bodies that were designed to twirl in freedom.

Adults don't tend to dance or twirl quite as freely, at least most of the time. Something happens to us along the way. Once embodied as children (for however short or long that may have been), we grow into dis-embodied beings for so many reasons. We live from the neck up without really exploring what it could mean to be wholly embodied, or in other words, present with our bodily feelings, sensations, and needs.

While our bodies aren't necessarily fragile, our connection with them often is. As the poet Jane Kenyon writes, it's often a "long struggle to be at home in the body."[1]

Pain in the body will draw our awareness back to the truth that we are bodied selves, whether we think of our lives that way or not. A stubbed toe will make us more conscious of our foot. A while back I slipped on some rocks at the beach and needed eight stitches to sew up a deep cut that ran right through my left eyebrow. My cheekbone was tender to the touch for months, and my forehead was itchy as the cut healed. The wound drew my focus to areas on my face I don't often consider.

Interestingly, emotional pain will do the same thing if we allow it. Yet because we are often dis-embodied, we notice only our emotional anguish in our mind without observing where it is being housed in the body. As with so many things in our lives, we don't explore beyond the surface until something underneath starts sending stress signals— whether our toes are swollen or we are doubled over in grief. It seems we are especially prone to need help in noticing our bodied selves.

———————

The practice of yoga has taught me to start observing my body a little more. Throughout the class, our instructor will often encourage us to breathe and be attentive. "Inhale, exhale," she prompts. "What do you notice in your body?" she asks. A few questions are helpful if we're willing to notice.

How are your grief and pain showing up in your body? Where is your body carrying them? Expressions like *he's a pain in the neck, that's a punch to the gut,* or *that's a real kick in the shins* communicate that what we feel emotionally also lands in our body. Grief, anguish, heartache, anxiety, or shame resonate within us in "bodied" ways, such as heaviness in our chest, tightness in our gut, trembling in our hands, or even a bracing in our posture. It isn't a bad thing that our bodies experience these sensations. It's a reminder that we are bodied people. In other words, we can't feel fear, for example, without a fearful sensation showing up physiologically. If we feel shame, we're likely to feel a warm flush come over us. Anger might land in a tight place in our chest, or a knot in the stomach can make itself known if we're anxious.

Ideally, we attune to any place in our bodies that is struggling and get curious about that sensation, wondering if it's a light flashing on our dashboard letting us know we need to tend to something. You can see how it becomes problematic if we're dis-embodied, not willing (or even aware) to look at what we're holding. We stay more "above the neck," and the emotions get lodged within. As the saying goes, "the issues are in the tissues." Of course, the more loss and grief we're experiencing, the more our bodies must handle.

A friend of mine experienced overwhelming heartache when her husband confessed his sexual addiction. Given their intense fears that he would lose his job should that information get out, they chose to go into seclusion with their pain. Within a few days, Ellen began to have a steady migraine that wouldn't go away. Various symptoms would ebb and flow. About the time she would think she was feeling a little better, she'd load her kids up in the car and head off to an errand, only to begin seeing double. Many times in that month she had to call someone to come get them. The neurologist referred to it as a "state of migraine," the same unrelenting headache for a month. Even though he asked, "Any idea what's triggered this?" Ellen still didn't feel like she could be honest with anyone. It would take traversing a difficult, lonely path for a season before Ellen and Rob found their way to a safe community.

"Trauma is not what happens to us, but what we hold inside in the absence of an empathetic witness," writes Gabor Mate.[2] Ellen desperately needed an empathetic witness to her pain but hadn't yet experienced where that kind of safety could be found. The chaos and anguish were exacerbated because of the trauma waging internally, clearly trying to make itself known in the form of a four-week headache. Community and connection with safe friends, a support group, and a therapist proved to be the framework Ellen needed to gain traction in her healing. Likewise, Rob found a recovery team as well, supporting him as he moved into active recovery.

Inhale. Exhale. What do you notice in your body? Those prompts always catch me off guard when my yoga instructor inserts them into the class. They feel random. And almost every time I realize I'm far more focused on "doing" a pose than being present in my body. Often I need the reminder to breathe.

In the Christian faith, we are familiar with the language of the body of Christ, maybe even to the point of moving too swiftly past the concept that the body of Christ was created to remind us of the *body* of Christ: the incarnation of God who became flesh and dwelt among us. We don't often think of bringing our bodies to the body; we tend to think of bringing our minds, our hearts, our pain, or our tithes and offerings. We need others in *the body* to help us navigate the heartache we feel in our own *bodies.* That might not be common thinking around these issues, but as reflected in an earlier chapter, we are designed in the likeness of the Trinity for community. To be well, we need the healing presence of others to help us release what we're carrying in our bodies.

It had long been a dream for my friends Ray and Evelyn to share living space with their daughter, Laura, and her family. Laura and her husband, Josh, welcomed Ray and Evelyn into their downstairs apartment, making it possible for them to have their own space while being near their daughter, son-in-law, and four grandchildren. The eight family members were finding the intergenerational arrangement meaningful, grateful for the connections that proximity provides. A few months in, the family turned in for the evening in the midst of an intense rainstorm. Deep in the night, one of the grandchildren came to rouse Ray and Evelyn from their sleep. "There's a fire," he said. "Take my hand. We've got to get out." What unfolded confounded their sense of how the world is supposed to work. Lightning had not only struck their home and started a massive fire but had hit four other homes in their small community. Without enough trucks from the volunteer fire department to cover all five fires and without enough water pressure between those they could reach, the family watched their home burn. As they stood on the porch with the family dog they'd adopted the night before, Josh continued to say: "We're all eight here. We're all eight here."

With deep thanks, Ray and Evelyn recount the gift that they all made it out alive that night. Evelyn shared that each of them remembered things or thought of ways to navigate the chaos as it unfolded. "We were given heightened abilities to think clearly that night," she shares. "I'm convinced it's one of the reasons our lives were spared."

As with most substantial things in life, this was a both/and. They live daily with a profound gratitude that they all survived the fire, and they regularly rely on their deep faith in God that has sustained them. That night also set in motion the constant change the family has been in for the two years since the night of the fire. Moving from their home to a hotel and several places since has required a continuous state of adjustment and so much loss of routine. It is difficult for anyone but is especially chaotic for those in their eighties. They've had to navigate so much trauma: losing all of their belongings, having everything change so quickly, and living with the postponement in the rebuilding of their home due to delays from the insurance company and the town where they live. From the night of the fire it was a painfully long two years before construction began to rebuild the home.

Yet as I talked with Ray and Evelyn, a sense of surrender and peace permeated the conversation. When I asked what's helped them navigate this, they begin to talk about their community of safe friends. "They felt our pain," Ray says. "Most of our friends have lived long enough to have had a lifetime of their own experiences. They understand tragedy, which allowed them to be comfortable with what to say and when to stop. Honestly, they didn't need to say much. They felt our pain and communicated it through their eyes, facial expressions, and tone of voice. There was a shared sense of understanding difficult experiences."

In *The Body Keeps the Score*, author and therapist Bessel van der Kolk writes of the power of safe community in helping our bodies navigate trauma:

> Numerous studies of disaster response around the globe have shown that social support is the most powerful protection against becoming overwhelmed by stress and trauma. Social support is not the same as merely being in the presence of others. The critical issue is *reciprocity*: being truly heard and seen by the people around us, feeling that we are held in someone else's

mind and heart. For our physiology to calm down, heal, and grow we need a visceral feeling of safety. No doctor can write a prescription for friendship and love: These are complex and hard-earned capacities.[3]

I read van der Kolk's words with deep gratitude for my friends, Ray and Evelyn. Their physiology has been allowed space to "calm down, heal, and grow," because of their safe community. And it was often the physical communication from others through kind eyes, empathetic facial expressions, or a gracious tone of voice that were the most significant avenues of that healing balm. They had empathetic witnesses for sure.

It's important to add this is a both/and: We absolutely need others to empathetically witness our pain. And we can learn to be kind, compassionate observers to our own heartache. We discover new language and develop the capacity to put a hand over our own hearts and say to ourselves, "Wow, that hurt. No wonder I'm in pain. This is tough." We learn to sit with God, the Man of Sorrows acquainted with grief, and hear God's voice say to us: "I see you, Beloved. I know this hurts." We need both to have others witnessing our pain and to see our own.

Inhale. Exhale. What do you notice in your body? As we learn to pay attention to how our grief and pain are held in our bodies, we have an opportunity to look more closely at how we engage our bodies overall.

Even before this current loss—how have you "noticed" your body? We trust that God has "knit us together in our mother's womb" (see Psalm 139:13), but we don't always like the shape of the body that resulted from that knitting—believing it to be too large, too short, too small in some places, or too unsightly in others. Quite possibly our bodies were the landscape on which such painful things as abuse, rape, or assault have occurred, so how we feel about them is understandably chaotic. Some of us were abandoned around issues with our bodies: not given important information about how it would grow and develop, left alone to understand what it meant to be sexually healthy, or in some cases, left without even our basic needs of food and clothing being met. It's possible we didn't get the physical affection we were designed to need. Currently, maybe we struggle with the fullness of our bodies such as our sensuality or our sexuality, so we shut that part of us down, rarely engage it, or misuse it. In some cases, we've taken Paul's metaphors too literally, believing that the spirit is "good" and the flesh is "bad"—and in an effort to honor God, we distance ourselves from our bodies. So many reasons exist for why we might move through life from the neck up, dis-embodied.

If you grew up in a home and/or church context that taught you to love and embrace your body in all of its goodness, bless those parents and church leaders for the gift they gave you. Many of us, though, either received things we didn't need or didn't hear some things that could have been valuable. When you trace back the history of how the church has handled the body, you find disturbing writings of theologians waging war against the body because of some of their own struggles. While the writings from the fourth century may seem far removed from us, it's helpful to recognize the legacy of unhealth around the body that we have inherited. That's especially incongruent given that Christianity is significantly *embodied:* Creation, incarnation, death, burial, resurrection, and the Eucharist. God created us as beings with bodies. God came in the form of a body.

While Jesus was on earth, power left his body to heal others. He wrapped his arms around children and used his hands to help people who were lame to walk and people who were crippled to stand. He mixed his saliva with mud to make a paste to heal a man's blindness, and he allowed a grateful woman to wash his feet. Jesus' body was crucified and died. His body rose again. Jesus gave us the Eucharist to remember: This is my body, eat. This is my blood, drink. *Creation, incarnation, crucifixion, resurrection, the Eucharist.* Ours is an embodied faith. Pastor Nadia Bolz-Weber offers this blessing for the body:

> The trauma your body holds can be metabolized into something else, something raised from soil like Jesus himself who showed his hands and his side to his faltering friends and said "peace be with you." Because God saves us *in* our bodies, not *from* our bodies and I want that knowledge to be a blessing. . . . If human bodies were anything less than holy, I don't think they would be where God chose to place God's image.[4]

Amen and amen.

Pain, trauma, grief, loss don't have to have the last word with our hearts and minds—or our stomachs, necks, shoulders, or any other places in our bodies where our pain gets lodged. They'll have a word, for sure. But not the last one. As Peter Levine says, "I believe not only that trauma is curable, but that the healing process can be a catalyst for profound awakening—a portal opening to emotional and genuine spiritual transformation."[5]

Clinically, this is known as posttraumatic *growth*. As my friend and colleague Debbie Laaser writes in her research, it's where trauma and transformation can coexist. We will be wounded, *and* we can heal. Posttraumatic growth is when a person who has experienced trauma discovers an appreciation for life, more compassion for others, trust in themselves that they can handle difficulties, growth in their relation-ships, and an ever-deepening faith.[6]

Ray and Evelyn experienced posttraumatic growth through the way they've developed the capacity to receive and not just give, for the oppor-tunities God is allowing them to share "comfort from the comfort they have received" to others who may be experiencing traumatic experi-ences. Theologically this is called resurrection. New life from the ashes.

Inhale. Exhale. What do you notice? Do you notice that what you're carrying in your body can calm down and be encouraged to heal with an empathetic witness? Do you notice that you are a bodied person, made in the image of the Creator who thought so highly of the body that Jesus came as a bodied person?

———————

Those same twin boys I spoke of earlier regularly make me laugh with their funny comments or responses. One day when I was talking with Ryder, Emmett's brother, he was surprised when I told him to be watch-ing for the mail carrier to bring birthday presents for him and Emmett. "Ohhh!" he said with a big smile. "That's unexpecting!" From that min-ute on, Greg and I adopted that phrase into our lexicon for when some-thing surprises us: *It's the fifth day in a row to have sunshine in typically gray Chicago winter.* "That's unexpecting!" *I went to the gym three times this week.* "That's unexpecting! *Our dog, Lucy, didn't snatch the cookies off the counter.* "That's unexpecting!"

For good reason, we expect loss to bring pain, suffering, and heart-ache. Yet it might surprise us that eventually, as we walk this journey, it can be an on-ramp toward more meaningful, holistic ways of living, including embracing our bodied selves. It may be that we've asked our bodies to hold our afflictive emotions without ever having an empathetic witness. Maybe we've waged war on our bodies for years or have been dis-embodied for a host of different reasons. Yet something in this season encourages us to soften, to welcome, and to be grateful for the truth that God came in a body to help us love our own.

Inhale. Exhale. That's unexpecting.

Spiritual Practice: Compassionate Body Scan

Find a comfortable chair and be seated. Allow yourself to ground yourself into your seat with your feet on the floor. Start by placing your palms face open in a receiving posture. Take a few deep breaths in and exhale fully. Begin with prayer, asking our kind and compassionate God to help you see your bodied self with a kind and compassionate lens.

Using your internal eye, start at the top of your head and move gently through the body. Pause and notice your head, mind, forehead, ears, eyes, nose, mouth, heart, shoulders, arms, stomach, hips, legs, feet, and so on. What compassion, kindness, or gratitude can you offer various body parts? If possible, move your hand to that part of your body and touch it softly with your palm. Here are some examples of ways to bless your body:

To your eyes: *You have cried a great number of tears in the last few months. It makes sense you're tired. Thank you for helping me move through this grief. I'm grateful you have allowed me to experience God's healing grace through the beauty of sunsets or blooming flowers.*

To your shoulders: *You have been carrying a heavy load. Thank you.*

To your heart: *You have been broken and the ache you feel is immense.*

To your mind: *Thank you for helping me be wise and clear in making good decisions in these difficult days.*

Maybe your noticing is broader, and you are prompted to express gratitude to your body for what it's done for you over the years:

To your feet: *Thank you for allowing me to walk and explore my neighborhood or hike in an international country when I travel.*

To your arms: *Thank you for allowing me to hug the ones I love. I'm grateful you help me to stay healthy by allowing me to ride a bike, paddle a kayak, or swing a tennis racket.*

To your hands: *I'm thankful you afford me the chance to engage hobbies that bring me fulfillment like cooking, photography, quilting, woodworking, or gardening.*

Another possibility is that you are aware of a sense of shame that arises in you as you attune to your body. As you are able, ask the Comforting One to guide you as you turn with compassion to those parts of your body that you have historically disliked, that you've been teased about, that you have been ashamed of or disappointed in. Allow time to be present with what gets stirred up in you and ask the Comforting One for the words to bless these parts of your body.

Give yourself an extended time (twenty minutes or so) to listen, observe, and notice. Allow Jesus, who came in a body, to help you compassionately see and be grateful for yours.

For more information, see Tara M. Owens, *Embracing the Body: Finding God in Our Flesh and Bone* (Downers Grove, IL: IVP Books, 2015).

ELEVEN

The Larger Story

*Storytelling always has been, and always will be one of
humanity's greatest tools for survival. But be warned. In
Scripture, and in life, the road to deliverance nearly always
takes a detour. Rarely do the people of God reach any kind
of promised land without a journey or two through the
wilderness.*

—Rachel Held Evans, *Inspired*

*So we fix our eyes not on what is seen, but on what is
unseen. For what is seen is temporary, but what is unseen in
eternal.*

—2 Corinthians 4:18, NIV

A few years ago, Sadie came to our support group broken and devastated. Her husband of ten years had been arrested and publicly fired from his ministerial position at their church. Even when he was out of the home, police came to their house and harassed her in front of her two young sons. The church stumbled in dealing with the crisis, at times being supportive and at other points adding unnecessary pain to an already excruciating situation. When Sadie and I met for the first time, she was physically upright but internally coiled into the fetal position. Her husband, Ben, was equally broken. From the beginning, he was remorseful and intentional to pursue his emotional work and healing—yet there was so much that had been betrayed.

From the start of our connection, I watched Sadie with interest. Her story was traumatic and public, with multiple layers of heartache. Despite the pain, I sensed she was "good for it"—meaning she had the hunger to be well and the commitment to pursue her healing. A few years down the road, Sadie's group welcomed a new member, and each took turns sharing their own story. When it was Sadie's turn, she bore witness to the agony she had known in her husband's explosion, yet there was more to the narrative:

> My story has many difficult pieces to it, and early on I thought this would be the only filter through which I would view my life. I would never have believed I could come to live a life in which I'm content, finding fulfillment, and even experiencing joy. And that doesn't mean I don't still have really tough days. But I was thrown into the deep end, and I'm learning I have buoyancy. It's impacted every area of my life from my parenting, my marriage, to my faith. I'm on a journey of looking at myself and exploring some work I didn't even realize I needed. I'm releasing what no longer works for me about my understanding of God, coming to embrace a more expansive view of the Divine as compassionate and kind—trusting that I'm truly beloved. What started out as so much awfulness has been surrounded by significant good.

One story, painful and heartbreaking, set down in a larger story that makes the first one more bearable. "All sorrows can be borne if you put them into a story or tell a story about them," said author Karen Blixen.[1] As I listened to Sadie that morning, I knew she was bearing her sorrow by the way she was telling her story, the pain *and* the good. Trusting that a greater story exists allows us to get out of bed in the morning, inviting us to the truth that maybe there's more going on than we can see in the midst of our pain. Rachel Held Evans noted, "As counselors and neuroscientists continue to confirm, the ability to shape a narrative from your experiences, and to connect your story to a greater one, is essential for developing empathy, a sense of purpose, and well-being."[2]

Understandably, Sadie couldn't have had that perspective at the beginning. Her pain was so intense it was largely impossible to see over the top of it. In fact, in my experience, it can be detrimental when we try to rush a person through their journey or explain away their hurt by quoting scripture that "God will work together all things for good." Yes, that's true, and thank God for it. And—what if it's a progression of perspective that quite possibly begins when God shares our sadness with us in whatever pain is unfolding?

Sadie was beginning to embrace the redemptive benefits of her pain, which don't diminish the agony but do make it a little more endurable. And just in case you're wondering, it's important to name that only seeing one dimension of this might sound something like "God allowed this for my self-improvement." When we begin to wrestle with that, we will understandably circle back and ask, *Wait . . . was there no other way to encourage my growth than this?* It is good and right that God can redeem our suffering and bring about endurance, character, and hope as scripture describes. But what if that's only part of the story, set down inside a larger one?

A few years ago, a catastrophic loss upended my friend and pastor, Lisa, when her twenty-six-year-old son, Billy, was killed in a motorcycle accident. For her, her husband, and their family, the pain was blinding. Billy's death left a huge hole and sent Lisa on a journey through the wilderness. As a friend and parishioner in her congregation, I watched with deep empathy and respect as she wrestled honestly with her grief, her questions about God, and her theology of suffering. Over the next few years, I saw Lisa becoming more centered and grounded. Her preaching reflected both her pain and her hope. She began to grapple with what she has described as a somewhat narrow view of how pain builds character. "If the death of my son is *only* about making me more resilient or for my self-improvement, I don't want any of that," she told me recently. "I'd rather have my son back. I'm weary of a false notion that some Christians seem to want to wear their pain like a badge that says, 'Look what a better Christian I'm becoming because of the hard things I've been through.' I don't want a badge. I want my son. But—if it's possible that my pain and suffering can be used for healing and redemption and restoration in others' lives—*that* I can sign up for."

It really is a progression of perspective. What if moving through and feeling our grief creates space for God to then lovingly use our pain to form and shape us? If we aren't doing our work to be well, we have nothing to offer anyone else. Some of the most destructive people I've known are those who've experienced deep loss and never sought healing for it. Instead they lead, parent, and operate out of their pain and the defense mechanisms they've fashioned to deal with it. Much damage can be done living that way. However, if we allow God to use our heartache to transform us, rather than transmitting our pain to others (as Richard Rohr says) we emerge as healthier and grounded people. And we can't take others where we ourselves are not willing to go. As I do the sacred work of forgiving, I can be a safe place for others to explore what that could look like for them. As I watch a mentor surrender into God's presence of *what is* and release what she can't control, I'm moved and challenged to do the same. My friend and colleague Mark Laaser often taught the "Nehemiah principle": When rebuilding the city of Jerusalem after its destruction, each family was instructed to begin by rebuilding in front of their own home—then help with the communal restoration where needed. We must restore our own infrastructure first when pain and loss take their toll. But it doesn't stop there. The larger story is that we are then called to help build up our community out of what we have been learning through our healing.

As I've listened to my friend Lisa develop her theology of suffering, this reality is what I've watched unfold. God uses our story for our own transformation—*and* that of others. This truth is seen in many different arenas: In the 12 Steps, the final step is to "carry the message to others." Paul encourages us to comfort others out of the comfort we ourselves have received (see 2 Corinthians 1:4). In Nehemiah, we're instructed to help restore the community.

———

As I think of my own story, I'm so aware of the depth of people in my life who were doing their own work and brought healing and restoration to mine. I had some dear friends who had been willing to go after the pain in their own lives and thus knew how to sit with me in my dark places. Mark and Debbie Laaser had a similar story to ours and made the choice to be a beacon of hope to others dealing with the fallout of betrayal and addiction. So many of the volunteers in the workshop I led at the time of our explosion had experiences of marital heartache and were on a journey of seeking emotional and relational health. Week after week, they showed up to help other couples who found themselves in deep weeds. In fact, most of the volunteers had come to the workshop years prior as participants. As they began to heal, they started to "comfort out of the comfort they had received." I'm forever grateful that's the community I was surrounded by in the early years of this journey. I see it as one of the many ways God loved me well and prepared a way for me.

And the concentric circles of those who impacted me were larger still. I was greatly encouraged by Jerry Sittser, an author I've never met who wrote in his book *A Grace Disguised* of his own catastrophic loss of three family members in one car accident. It became a vision for me of moving through my own loss with hope that there really could be a larger story. And further out even still, Saint John of the Cross wrote in the sixteenth century of the "dark night of the soul," making known the truth that sometimes dark empty places in our lives make room for a union with the Divine Light that nothing else really could. I am comforted and encouraged to know that a great cloud of witnesses has gone before me to provide such handrails in dark hallways. Part of the larger story is the truth that I'm not alone in my suffering. It draws me up and invites me to look to the broader truth that my current loss is one chapter, not the whole story.

But if we have difficulty seeing the larger story, we aren't alone. So many biblical characters similarly struggled. The woman at the well believed Jesus was talking about something she could literally drink instead of something so much greater. The Israelites resisted trusting that God was leading them to freedom by way of the Exodus. It's so easy to be blinded by our pain and/or our immediate needs and thus be short-sighted. God keeps calling us to a perspective that is larger, wider, and higher.

————————

When my boys were younger, we had a tradition that every so often I would take them each out of school to do something fun together. Once, after checking my older son, Jacob, out of class, we made a glorious amount of popcorn and settled in to watch the first of the three Lord of the Rings movies, *The Fellowship of the Ring.* At the time, the other two movies hadn't been released, but Jacob had read the books and was eager for me to see the movie with him. I lost track of time and was truly surprised when the movie was over. "That's how this ends?" I asked. "That's abrupt! And it doesn't make any sense to end there!"

"That's not the end, Mom," he said. "Remember, it's not really three books. It's one. This is just part of the story. You should read them."

I suppose I was lazy and just waited for the other two movies to be released, but he was right. A much larger story unfolded of Sam and Frodo and the good and evil waged in Middle Earth. Battles were fought, a ring was destroyed, fantastical creatures rescued wounded hobbits, and several characters sailed off to the Undying Lands. J. R. R. Tolkien knew well that the best way to spin a tale is to set one down inside another.

Walter Bruggeman suggests that good theology is rooted in story: the idea that God is embedded in a narrative, and knowing God apart from that story isn't possible. "The narrative matrix of YHWH, the God of Israel, is the exodus narrative. This is the God 'who brought you out of the land of Egypt, out of the house of slavery.'"[3] The larger story, maybe the greatest story, is the overarching trajectory as told in the "exodus narrative." The scripture isn't just a compilation of multiple stories. We do well to remember that the various stories come together to form one account: that we are being drawn out of bondage toward freedom found in Divine Love. "It is for freedom that Christ has set free" (Gal. 5:1, NIV), as Paul tells us.

It's so easy for us to be engrossed in our current situation that we don't see the larger matrix of the "exodus narrative" that God is unfolding. Yet what if the mystery of God is woven directly into this all-encompassing story of how God moves God's children from slavery to freedom? And your story—and mine—are not happening outside of that narrative but *right in the midst of it*—one story set down inside another. We may easily feel confused, as I did watching *The Fellowship of the Ring*, wondering, *how does this make sense?* because we're focused on only one piece of the narrative. But what if there really is a larger picture, a more loving trajectory than at first glance?

Recently I was introduced to the Jewish concept of "black fire" and "white fire" with regard to the Torah. Rabbi Shimon b. Lakish developed this idea in the third century CE. He described the black letters and words on the pages as the "black fire," while "white fire" is designated as the space behind and in between the text itself. The black fire represents those things said, while the white embodies what is not said yet must be understood. One writer said of the "white fire," the "silent white parchment beneath the black ink represents the non-verbal depth and sanctity of God's revealed word."[4]

When we consider our own stories, it is understandable that we may only see the "black fire"—the facts of what happened, the concrete, confusing, maybe even complex details that surround us. And just like in the Torah, the stories can be both beautiful and painful. We read of the creation of the world, Cain murdering his brother, and Joseph forgiving his. Narratives unfold of how Moses was rescued as an infant, led the people out of slavery, and was not allowed into the Promised Land. Similarly, our stories are bursting with examples of pain and complication, beauty and redemption. That is the text of the story, our black fire, but maybe the larger story is remembering the white fire as well. What else must be understood? What is the nonverbal depth of God's revealed word, the space in which this text unfolded?

By its very nature, white fire is quiet, mysterious, or even silent. And yet we trust its presence—even if we don't realize it. We can't read the unfolding story without the white space behind it. If we see our stories through the lens of God's drawing us into freedom, then it allows the possibility that the white fire leaves space for the various ways that God is moving us forward in love, in the midst of our pain, in the middle of our heartaches, and even through our wildernesses.

Rather than allowing our response to our pain and grief to cause a second death in us, we move toward the freedom that healthy grieving ushers in. Instead of being enslaved to our "programs for happiness that inevitably don't work," we are invited to the freedom of finding our true selves. Instead of feeling bound to respond to our current situation in the same exact way we have been for months or years, we move into the freedom of knowing we have options. Instead of staying on the surface of our lives, we are invited to move toward the center of wholeness. Instead of being enslaved by old core beliefs (about ourselves, about those we love, about grief and suffering, or about God), we are walking into the freedom of knowing that we are loved and that *that* is our larger story.

Daily, regularly, we are invited to move "out of the house of slavery" of that which binds us and toward the freedom of our gracious God. In fact, telling the stories of God's faithfulness to that end is our heritage of faith:

> When your children ask you in time to come, "What is the meaning of the decrees and the statutes and the ordinances that the LORD our God has commanded you?" then you shall say to your children, "We were Pharaoh's slaves in Egypt, but the LORD brought us out of Egypt with a mighty hand. The LORD displayed before our eyes great and awesome signs and wonders against Egypt, against Pharaoh and all his household. He brought us out from there in order to bring us in, to give us the land that he promised on oath to our ancestors. Then the LORD commanded us to observe all these statutes, to fear the LORD our God, for our lasting good, so as to keep us alive, as is now the case. (Deut. 6:20-24)

So, if "storytelling has always been and will always be one of humanity's greatest tools for survival," let us tell our stories of what God is bringing us *out of* and calling us *into*. In safe community, let us be seen and known as we listen to and know others. When we can't see the bigger picture for the pain of the current one, let us help one another along the journey by embracing the freedom that it's okay (at least for now) not to understand as we seek to fix our eyes on what is unseen. Others around us can hold hope that God will waste nothing and can redeem our loss. May we trust that if we are in a wilderness of our own making or because of other things that have happened to us or around us, then we can be open (or at least open to being open) that somehow, someway, freedom in Divine Love is always, *always*, the trajectory of the larger story. "For it is for freedom that Christ has set us free" (Gal. 5:1, NIV).

Recently I listened to a sermon by Rev. Judy Petersen in which she referenced the story of the paralytic at the pool of Bethesda. She reflected that it would have made sense for the man, once healed, to leave behind the mat that symbolized his paralysis. He no longer needed it now that he could walk. Wouldn't it have been understandable if he wanted to rid himself of it? It probably stunk and was certainly a symbol of the many years he was crippled. But that isn't what Jesus instructed. "Jesus said to him, 'Stand up, take your mat and walk.' At once the man was made well, and he took up his mat and began to walk" (John 5:8-9). The mat, Petersen emphasized, "is the witness to where we've come from. It's a testimony to all that God has done. It's the shame we've come through that has been redeemed."[5]

My story has had many places of heartache with so many more strangely wrapped gifts along the way. And part of my larger story is that I have been taking up my mat and walking into freedom—freedom in my life and the hope that it may point others to freedom as well. I can leave behind emotional and spiritual paralysis (or continue to shed it) and take up my mat as a remembrance of all that God has done and continues to do in my life. Whether it's the story of my marriage or other formational experiences that have come my way, I don't leave my story behind. I take it with me. Not in a way that clings to shame, though. Rather, one that lives fully into the truth that Jesus has said to me, "Daughter: Stand up. Take your mat and walk."

That story of the paralytic begins with Jesus asking the man if he wants to be well. It's a fair question for each of us to consider. But maybe more important is the *One* asking the question. Jesus asked because he knew it was possible to be well. It's possible for us to experience growth after our trauma, resurrection after death and burial. The story isn't only about what's happened to us, it's about what happens *in* us . . . and what happens next.

Courage, dear heart, as you pick up your mat and walk.

Spiritual Practice: Reframing

When we change the mat or a frame around a piece of art or photo, it inevitably changes our view. Things we hadn't noticed before start coming into focus. Other aspects of the work fade into the background.

The spiritual practice of reframing is an invitation to allow God to reframe how you've been seeing your story and eventually welcome any different perspectives. But the goal isn't just a cognitive shift. It's prayer that invites God to reframe your felt sense of your story as well.

In a time of prayer, imagine yourself sitting with the Trinity. Maybe you're around a table together—or possibly you see yourself in the middle of the Three. Allow the Spirit to guide you as you imagine what each member of the Trinity may say to you or how each member engages you. Attune to your heart and body, noticing what you sense and hear as you are present in Community.

Considering the following questions as you sit with the Trinity. Notice who you are drawn to as you ask these questions . . . maybe it's all, maybe it's a particular member of the Trinity:

- How are you inviting me to understand my story in light of the larger story?
- If I've been stuck on the specifics of what's happened in my story, what are some ways you have been at work in the background (the "white fire") that I've not yet been willing/able to see?

- What is a different, larger perspective than the one I'm stuck on? Can you help me to reframe my understanding of what's happened? Of me, others, or you?
- What are you wanting to form and shape in me? To birth anew in me?
- How are you redeeming my story?
- How can I more deeply connect to your heart, God?
- How are you inviting me to pick up my mat and walk?

APPENDIX A:
DEPRESSION AND TRAUMA

One of the ways we can care for ourselves in the midst of profound grief is to normalize the experiences of depression and trauma. Given the loss you are facing, it is quite likely you will feel depressed at some point; likewise, trauma almost always accompanies loss. It's helpful to name that and look for it—and to know *you're not doing anything wrong* if you feel depressed or traumatized. It's usually not a matter of *if*; it's a question of *to what degree am I feeling depressed and experiencing trauma?*

In light of your loss, getting therapeutic help will be important. Honestly, I've never met anyone navigating deep pain that didn't need the support of good counseling. A good counselor can help you with processing your loss, healthy grieving, discerning how this may connect to more historical pain in your story, and determining how to move forward.

Depression[1]

If you feel depressed, a counselor can help you determine if you are moving through deep grief or if you've shifted into a more serious degree of depression that needs additional support. For example, some of the symptoms of grief and clinical depression are similar, such as excessive crying, difficulty concentrating, high anxiety, sleeplessness, or feeling void and empty. But one of the hallmarks of depression is when those experiences are accompanied by an inability to take care of yourself physically, get out of bed, and/or perform daily tasks for two weeks or more. A therapist can help you with the right next steps if you find yourself there. You may also need a doctor to help treat your symptoms if necessary.

Here is a quick online assessment that can help you determine where you are on the scale of depression. It is not designed to be a diagnosis but to give you a framework for understanding where you are. Again, the best support is with your professional therapist. https://www.depressioncenter.org/patient-health-questionnaire-phq-9

Finally, if you are struggling with thoughts of harming yourself or someone else, it's critical to seek help immediately by calling 911.

Trauma[2]

We tend to associate trauma only with soldiers returning from war or people who have experienced profound childhood abuse. While those experiences are definitely traumatic, trauma also shows up in a multitude of less obvious ways, such as the following:

- death of a loved one
- a serious injury (physical or emotional)
- a major accident or medical procedure
- witnessing any kind of violence
- being in a relationship with someone who is mentally/physically/emotionally abusive
- being regularly shamed or insulted by a parent or some other authority figure
- not receiving the care and nurture we needed as a child
- living in an unsafe environment
- intrusive, unwanted thoughts about a traumatic event

A saying in trauma-informed communities is "trauma is in the eye of the beholder." Basically, if it was traumatic for you, then you've experienced trauma. And doesn't that make sense? What may be traumatic for me, given my story, might not be as traumatic for another because of their history and life experiences. As with depression, a therapist can help you navigate your situation and address what you're facing in the best way possible. We know we need to address our trauma when we are experiencing any of the following:

- an inability to remember certain aspects of the event
- persistent inability to experience positive emotions
- irritability and angry outbursts
- sleep disturbances (sleeping too much or insomnia)
- avoiding people/places/reminders with anything associated with the trauma
- reckless behavior
- hypervigilance
- persistent negative beliefs about oneself, others, or the world in general

Consider the degree to which you have experienced trauma. If you are struggling to adjust to the many stressors it has caused, take good care of yourself and seek professional help. The earlier you can move into getting support, the less time there is to internalize the trauma, lowering its long-term impact. Thankfully, we are becoming a more trauma-literate society, and many therapists and clinicians are well trained to help you walk this journey as you seek to heal from your trauma.

Don't go this road alone. Build a strong support system around you. You are worth taking good care of.

APPENDIX B:
SMALL GROUP
DISCUSSION GUIDE

W*hat Loss Can Teach Us* can be a helpful book for support groups addressing losing a loved one or recovering from divorce. It would also be beneficial for a support group dealing with addiction or for spouses dealing with betrayal. Several questions have been provided for each chapter; some of them will pertain to certain losses better than others. Choose what works best for your group. These questions can also be helpful for individual use.

If using this in a group, consider sharing together in some of the spiritual practices found at the end of the chapters or in appendix C. It can be meaningful to experience *visio divina* (chapter 5) or *lectio divina* (chapter 8) in community. It can also work well for group members to practice dialogue journaling (chapter 2) or writing laments (see appendix C) and then share their writings with one another. Maybe you share songs from your grieving playlist (appendix C) during some group meetings.

Introduction and Chapter 1: Good Grief

1. How do you respond to the paradigm that "new life starts in the dark"? What emotions does that stir in you?
2. What are some ways that unprocessed grief shows up in you?
3. Are "warning lights" of contempt, resentment, or bitterness flashing on your dashboard? If so, what messages do they carry? What do those feelings want you to pay attention to?

4. What are some ways you avoid feeling grief or pain?

5. If any of your pain is leaking, where or on whom is it leaking?

6. In what ways is grief or pain being held in your body? What are you noticing?

7. While the grieving process isn't linear, where do you think you may be in the death, burial, and resurrection process?

8. What would it look like to move toward your pain in love?

9. Is there a need for sorrowful acceptance?

Chapter 2: God as Midwife, Not Rescuer

1. Have you believed that your relationship with God would protect you from painful things? If so, where do you think that belief originated?

2. Have you wanted/needed to ask God, "Where were you?" or "Why didn't you intervene?" If so, do you feel the freedom to do so?

3. If faith is a continuum of belief, doubt, and sacred ambiguity, where do you suppose you are on that continuum?

4. What are some "why" questions you've wanted to ask?

5. Are you open/willing to transition into asking "what" questions? If so, what are those questions? ("What do you want to form and shape in me?" "What are you surfacing?")

6. Talk about your image of God and where you suppose that originated. Do you gravitate more toward seeing God as a rescuer or as a midwife?

7. If you are open to seeing God in the business of midwifery rather than rescuing, what might God want to bring forth in you?

8. How are your current grief and pain inviting you to a different view of God?

Chapter 3: Remain in My Love

1. Has this loss caused you in any way to question your lovability?

2. Has this loss caused you to question God's goodness? If so, how?

3. What core beliefs do you have about yourself? About God?

4. Have you believed your identity is grounded in the "unstable sand" of your actions or performance?

5. How do you respond to the idea of God's blessing?

6. What's the narrative you live by? The tape you listen to?

7. What do you suppose God feels and thinks when you come to God's mind?

8. If you hustle for your worth, what shape does that take?

9. In what ways are you like the younger brother? The older one?

10. What do you suppose is your "far country" where you wander from home?

11. In what ways do you experience resentment like the older brother?

12. How might it affect you if you were to agree to the blessing God has for your life?

13. In what ways are you on a journey of becoming more loving? If your response is, "I'm not," what is underneath that?

Chapter 4: It's a Both/And

1. In what ways do you suppose you're applying either/or thinking to your current situation? To yourself? To God?

2. Have you been trying to apply logic to an illogically painful, heartbreaking reality? If so, what impact is that having?

3. How do you respond to the idea that one of the markers of emotional adulthood is learning to live in the tension of seemingly opposite things?

4. If you were to craft a both/and statement about your current situation that represents the fullness of the truth of your life right now, what would that be? (There can be more than one!)

5. How do you respond to the suggestion that heaven is here and now *and* there and then?

6. If paradox is the only thing large enough to help us navigate the messy and mysterious issues in life, where are you most needing the both/and right now in matters of grief, suffering, or love?

Chapter 5: Olly Olly Oxen Free

1. Can you describe a time when safe community has helped you "see your own face?"
2. What kind of "host" are you for yourself? Demanding? Critical? Absent? Gracious?
3. What kind of "host" are you for others? Demanding? Critical? Absent? Gracious?
4. How are you at learning to name your needs? How are you at asking others what they need?
5. How would you describe what it feels like to be truly heard and understood? Who in your life has listened well to you?
6. How are you doing in the process of seeking to become a safe listener (versus someone who hurries another into being quiet because what they're saying creates anxiety for you)?
7. How do you respond to the idea that, since we are made in the image of the Trinity, community is our *design?* What implications does that have for how you want to live your life?
8. With whom do you need to "stay at the table" in working to resolve a disconnection? God? Yourself? Your spouse? A friend or family member?

Chapter 6: Clean Anger

1. If you have any feelings of anger (anywhere from frustration to rage), what happens when you slow down and give your anger respect and attention? What message do you think the anger has for you?
2. What is your history with anger? How was it expressed (or stuffed/avoided) in your home growing up? What were the family rules (stated or unstated) about it?
3. How do you respond to the idea of "clean anger"?
4. What are your reflections about this statement from Harriet Lerner: "It actually takes great courage and vulnerability to get clear about our anger, to come out from behind the 'safe' wall

of inexpression and voice clearly and plainly what we are angry about"?

5. Do you gravitate more toward sadness (with the possibility of anger underneath) or more toward anger (with the possibility of sadness underneath)? Why do you suppose one of those is easier for you than the other?

6. How do you respond to the idea that clean anger can create intimacy rather than distance in our relationships?

7. When your anger is not coming across cleanly, how is it most likely to come across? Does it leak out in comments that are sarcastic, passive-aggressive, snarky, guilt producing, or nagging? Does it seep inward, leading to bitterness, contempt, and/or depression? Is it expressed in physical or verbal rage?

8. In ways that are responsible, kind, and clear, what do you need to get really mad about?

9. Given the current situation you're facing, are there some historic stories you're reminded of that have given you reasons to be angry?

10. How does the idea of transformational swearing land in you?

11. Do you have a desire/need to find a "clean" way to offload some anger (like throwing plates or eggs)?

Chapter 7: Take Off That Ugly Sweater: A Look at Shame

1. Which of the items on the list of things we can feel shame about resonate with you? Is there something not listed there that can trigger shame in you?

2. How do you suppose shame is showing up for you? Do you have grief shame? Are you over-qualifying something? Are you second-guessing yourself frequently?

3. Have you (even if just in your mind) shamed another from a place of self-righteousness? What did that sound like? Who are you most likely to shame?

4. In what ways did you experience shame growing up in your family, at school, in your community, or at church?

5. Where are you in the process of developing a sense of shame resiliency?

6. Are you wearing a cloak of shame, an "ugly sweater"? Who in your life can help you take that off?

7. The next time you're in a shame storm, what words from Jesus would be helpful?

Chapter 8: It's a Marathon, Not a Sprint

1. Do you believe you've had some misconceptions about what forgiveness is or isn't? How has that affected you?

2. How do you respond to the idea of forgiveness being a marathon with multiple laps rather than a quick sprint down the track?

3. What would it mean for you if forgiveness was a progressive process rather than a one-time event?

4. Do you suppose you are experiencing unforgiveness toward someone?

5. If you consider forgiveness to be engaging "liminal space," what do you suppose God wants to transform in you?

6. Is there a hurt in your life that has been your "final home"? In other words, are you stuck in the woundedness of it rather than moving toward forgiveness?

Chapter 9: Welcoming What Is

1. Is there something in your life that you've been internally (or externally) stomping around about, refusing to accept?

2. What affect would it have in your life if you were to be accept the reality of *what is*?

3. In what ways have you seen God in what is?

4. If/when you are resistant to accepting what is, what are the old coping mechanisms that your "survivor" tends to use to defend yourself from feeling pain?

5. What is your image of God? Is there any part of that god that you need to "fire"?

6. How do you feel about the idea that "Jesus is what God has to say"?

7. What would it look like to relinquish into a place of trust and surrender rather than digging into a place of resistance?

Chapter 10: Embracing Our Bodies

1. How and where do you suppose the pain and grief of your loss is showing up in your body?
2. Who has been a witness to your pain, helping your physiology to calm down, heal, and grow?
3. Historically, how have you viewed your body? What emotions have you had about it?
4. How does the fact that Jesus came as a bodied person affect how you see your own body?
5. How are you experiencing posttraumatic growth? Are you discovering more compassion for others? Trusting that you can handle difficult things? Experiencing an ever-deepening faith?

Chapter 11: The Larger Story

1. How do you respond to the idea that some redemptive benefits could come from this pain? That a larger story, a broader narrative could exist? In other words, what do you suppose this loss has to teach you?
2. Given the deep pain that has come your way and thrown you into the deep end, how are you experiencing buoyancy? If you're drowning, what do you need to help you stay afloat in this pain?
3. In what ways can your story be used redemptively in the lives of others? In other words, how could you eventually provide comfort out of the comfort you have received?
4. In what ways is God calling you toward freedom as you move through your grief?
5. Is there part of your story that you're ashamed of? What would it mean to pick up your mat and take it with you as you walk into freedom?
6. Consider finding some meaningful ways to say to one another in your group: Take up your mat and walk!

APPENDIX C:
ADDITIONAL SPIRITUAL
PRACTICES FOR LOSS

S piritual practices are a vehicle for us to find our way to presence with ourselves as we seek to be with Presence. While each of the chapters has at least one suggested spiritual practice, the following are additional recommendations for engaging God in times of loss, pain, grief, or on a day of just needing to be reminded that God is bigger than this (whatever the "this" happens to be at the time).

In his beautiful book *Emotionally Healthy Spirituality*, Peter Scazzero shares a story often told about cold, snowy climates. In the season of blinding snowstorms, people would need to get from their home to their barn to care for animals during a blizzard. Tragically, the intense storm would sometimes disorient a farmer so badly that he would be found dead just a few feet from his front door, unable to find his way back home. The practice developed of tying a rope from the house to the barn as a safe way to travel between the two even in a blizzard. Spiritual practices are a rope of sorts. The practices themselves aren't home, but they lead us there, especially in times of blinding storms.

1. **Written Lament**: Although it may not be the first thing we think of when we consider the Psalms, more laments than praises make up this book of the Bible. Lament is an important part of authentically showing up with ourselves and with God.

   Often, laments have three parts:

A. Naming what is wrong/expressing what we're grieving/ crying out with our sorrow

B. Naming how we want God to move

C. Expressing the truth of God's faithfulness and goodness

Notice the structure of excerpts from Psalm 10, for example:

Why, O Lᴏʀᴅ, do you stand far off?
Why do you hide yourself in times of trouble? (verse 1) *(Crying out to God)*

Rise up, O Lᴏʀᴅ; O God, lift up your hand;
do not forget the oppressed (verse 12) *(Naming how we want God to move)*

O Lᴏʀᴅ, you will hear the desire of the meek;
you will strengthen their heart, you will incline your ear
to do justice for the orphan and the oppressed,
so that those from earth may strike terror no more (verses 17-18) *(Expressing the truth of God's faithfulness and goodness)*

Consider an example of a personal lament:
Why do you seem so far away, God? Why did you not intervene to stop this from happening? My "enemies" of depression, guilt, and regret are haunting me. *(Crying out to God)*

Emmanuel, make yourself known in ways that are clear, tangible, and undeniable. *(Naming how you want God to move)*

I trust that you are good and faithful even if I cannot see it clearly now *(Expressing the truth of who God is)*

Write your own lament using the above format.

2. **Visceral Lament**: At the end of chapter 6, *Clean Anger*, the spiritual practice of plate throwing is recommended. Sometimes our grief and pain need a physical outlet, providing that we are not

hurting someone, ourselves, or property that we care about. The goal is to offload that angry energy as we find our way to healing and freedom. You may find it helpful to do the following:

A. Silent Scream. This is a great way to engage the anger in your grief, "screaming" with your diaphragm and breath but not engaging your vocal cords.

B. Take an old book or catalog and write a word or phrase on each of the pages then rip them up.

C. On sticky notes, write down things that you are angry about, placing the sticky notes all over an old bed or couch. A word or short phrase is all that's needed. Using a tennis racket, plastic bat, or broom handle, express your anger through hitting the sticky notes.

3. **Praying with Feelings**. See if you can imagine an image for your afflictive emotion, such as grief, pain, disgust, anxiety, fear, terror, or sadness. Maybe it's a shape, color, or certain texture. Then give the image a voice. Dialogue, allowing a conversation to unfold between you and the feeling. What do you notice? What does it need? What does it want to say? Does it have a message from your soul? Invite the Wonderful Counselor to bring discernment and wisdom as you listen to your feelings.

4. **Tea or Coffee?** Sometimes there is a part of ourselves that has been inaccessible or that we don't like. It can be overwhelming to consider embracing that part of ourselves. A safe and loving practice is learning to wade in slowly and have "coffee or tea" with that part of us. It's short, limited, and boundaried. We learn to ask ourselves, *Can I be open enough for a little while to create a space to talk to that part of me or to allow it to talk with me?* Be a gracious host and invite that part of you to have coffee or tea. In a posture of imaginative prayer, sit a while and see what you notice. Consider inviting a member of the Trinity to join you as well.

5. **Enneagram.** The Enneagram is a tremendous tool for personal and spiritual transformation. Organized into nine types, it is a personality type system that helps us understand the defense mechanisms of our false selves and the path toward becoming

conscious and aware of who we can be in our true selves as God created. Multiple resources are available such as *The Road Back to You* by Ian Morgan Cron and Suzanne Stabile, *The Sacred Enneagram* by Chris Heuertz, www.enneagraminstitutute.com, and *The Enneagram: A Christian Perspective* by Richard Rohr and Andreas Ebert.

6. **Touchstones.** Set up an altar (in your home or in a garden) with a few things that remind you of what is good, such as a rock, seashell, a picture, a painting, a plant, etc. Consider sitting at the altar in prayerful presence and holding an object from the altar that brings you back to a safe space.

7. Consider searching for a **Spiritual Companion, Guide, or Director**—someone who will hold space for you as you listen for God's movement.

8. **Grieving Playlist**. Music will move us and evoke feelings in ways that few other things can. Consider creating a playlist that aligns with your tastes and invites you to be present. As said elsewhere, the goal is not to manufacture emotions; rather, it's to call forth what you need to befriend and release. This will be **unique** to you: It could be anything from Broadway to Rap, Classical to Country. Maybe it's pipe organ, bagpipes, or electric guitar. The idea is to form a playlist that helps you let down and be present.

Some suggestions:
- Something majestic like Bach's Cello Suite No. 1 in G Major, Prelude or Edward Elgar's *Enigma Variations*, Variation IX (Adagio) "Nimrod"
- Traditional hymns like "Come Thou Fount," "It Is Well With My Soul," or "Be Thou My Vision." Find versions that are meaningful to you.
- Christian artists you have resonated with. Maybe that includes musicians like Chris Rice, Kari Jobe, Sarah Groves, Audrey Assad, Kathryn Scott, Kings Kaleidoscope, or Maverick City.

- Secular music that calls deep within you, and the louder it gets the more you awake to what you are feeling. Maybe the songs stir you to cry, yell, dance, or scream/sing (yes, that's a thing). This could be any artist from Kendrick Lamar to Queen to Johnny Cash—whatever engages your emotions.
- Broadway tunes (and if that sounds strange, listen to "For Good" from *Wicked*)
- Songs from movie soundtracks like "This Is Me" from *The Greatest Showman* or "Gabriel's Oboe" by Ennio Moriconne from *The Mission*
- Instrumental music like quiet piano, cello, or acoustic guitar

Important Note: One of our biggest fears is that once we find our way to our sorrow, we won't be able to pull ourselves back out and go on with our day/work/take the kids to school. Music is great for that transition too. Consider songs that help you take a deep breath and then trust you'll be able to take the next step. Maybe they make you smile; perhaps you love to sing along and harmonize; maybe they remind you of your youth. Create the "All Shall Be Well/I've Got to Get Back to Work" playlist too.

APPENDIX D:
JOURNEYING WITH OUR
GRIEF THROUGH MOVIES

ometimes we are open (or at least open to being open) to feeling
our grief or sadness, only to discover that it is lodged within
us. Our bodies feel weighed down and heavy under the load of
emotion. It can be helpful to create some pathways to help those afflictive
emotions find their way to the surface. Movies can be a helpful tool to
get the logjam moving.

Sometimes, watching movies that depict a situation similar to what
we are dealing with can allow us to access our own grief. At other times,
we need to watch a movie about a different kind of grief from what we
are facing. The sadness is similar enough to stir our lodged emotions
without being too close to home and offending our sense of well-being.
It's a "back door" into our sense of loss. Still another option is watching
a positive depiction of something we didn't experience to help us access
our grief over what we haven't had.

This practice is not about manufacturing emotions. Rather, it's a way
to honor your heart and soul and listen to what is yours. You would not
feel it if it were not yours to feel. As you watch, consider what the reality is
within you that is resonating with the story.

It's important to note that some of these movies may not be to your
taste or fit your worldview. Some have adult themes or adult language
and would not be good for younger audiences. Be sure to note the rating
of any movie before watching it. Take what's yours and leave the rest.

Movies dealing with childhood abandonment, neglect, feeling lost, trying to heal

- *Dead Poets Society* (1989)
- *Good Will Hunting* (1997)
- *The Hours* (2002)
- *Life as a House* (2001)
- *Lion* (2016)
- *Secondhand Lions* (2003)

Romantic, sad movies

- *Atonement* (2007)
- *The Fault in Our Stars* (2014)
- *Legends of the Fall* (1994)
- *The Notebook* (2004)
- *A Star Is Born* (2018)
- *Titanic* (1997)

Movies dealing with longing for a parent connection

- *Big Fish* (2003)
- *The Descendants* (2011)
- *Field of Dreams* (1989)
- *Manchester by the Sea* (2016)
- *Onward* (2020)

Movies dealing with saying goodbye or grieving a transition

- *The Best Exotic Marigold Hotel* (2011)
- *E.T. the Extra-Terrestrial* (1982)
- *Forrest Gump* (1994)
- *Inside Out* (2015)
- *The Lord of the Rings: The Return of the King* (2003)
- *Toy Story 3* (2010)

Movies involving animals

- *Charlotte's Web* (2006)
- *A Dog's Purpose* (2017)
- *Hachi: A Dog's Tale* (2009)
- *Into the Wild* (2007)
- *Marley & Me* (2008)

Movies dealing with trauma/loss from war

- *Born on the Fourth of July* (1989)
- *Life Is Beautiful* (1997)
- *The Pianist* (2002)
- *Sarah's Key* (2010)
- *Schindler's List* (1993)

Movies dealing with loss of a sibling

- *Ordinary People* (1980)
- *The Secret Life of Bees* (2008)

Movies dealing with breaking down barriers

- *12 Years a Slave* (2013)
- *The Butterfly Circus* (2009; short film)
- *Just Mercy* (2019)
- *Moonlight* (2016)
- *The Peanut Butter Falcon* (2019)
- *Selma* (2014)
- *Yentl* (1983)

Movies dealing with loss of a spouse

- *P.S. I Love You* (2007)
- *Shadowlands* (1993)
- *Up* (2009)
- *We Bought a Zoo* (2011)

Movies dealing with loss of a child

- *Lorenzo's Oil* (1992)
- *Ordinary People* (1980)
- *Rabbit Hole* (2010)
- *The Shack* (2017)
- *Steel Magnolias* (1989)
- *The Way* (2010)

Movies dealing with losing a parent

- *Coco* (2017)
- *Extremely Loud & Incredibly Close* (2011)
- *Troop Zero (2019)*

Movies that depict connection within families

- *About a Boy* (2002)
- *About Time* (2013)
- *August: Osage County* (2013)
- *Brave* (2012)
- *Little Women* (2019)
- *Yours, Mine & Ours* (2005)

Movies that represent meaningful friendships/ community/being a part of a team

- *Beaches* (1988)
- *The Breakfast Club* (1985)
- *The Butterfly Circus* (2009; short film)
- *Finding Nemo* (2003)
- *Fried Green Tomatoes* (1991)
- *Me and Earl and the Dying Girl* (2015)
- *Rudy* (1993)
- *School of Rock* (2003)
- *The Shawshank Redemption* (1994)
- *Stand by Me* (1986)
- *Steel Magnolias* (1989)

- *Toy Story* (1995)

Movies that depict forgiveness

- *Chocolat* (2000)
- *Lady Bird* (2017)
- *Jirga* (2018)
- *An Unfinished Life* (2005)

This list is a compilation of ideas from multiple spiritual directors, friends, and family. For additional resources, see https://www.spiritual-ityandpractice.com/films for a thorough list of emotionally literate films to support your spiritual journey.

APPENDIX E:
SUGGESTED READING

Reading can be an important tool in the work of emotional and spiritual health. Below you'll find suggestions to support you in your journey. Far better than reading widely is reading deeply. Allow the works time and space to invite, stir, challenge, and comfort you.

Naming the truth of your identity as a beloved child of God

- *Abba's Child: The Cry of the Heart for Intimate Belonging* by Brennan Manning
- *The Inner Voice of Love: A Journey Through Anguish to Freedom* by Henri J. M. Nouwen
- *Life of the Beloved: Spiritual Living in a Secular World* by Henri J. M. Nouwen
- *Original Blessing: Putting Sin in Its Rightful Place* by Danielle Shroyer
- *The Return of the Prodigal Son: A Story of Homecoming* by Henri J. M. Nouwen
- *Sinners in the Hands of a Loving God: The Scandalous Truth of the Very Good News* by Brian Zahnd
- *Surrender to Love: Discovering the Heart of Christian Spirituality* by David G. Benner
- *Tattoos on the Heart: The Power of Boundless Compassion* by Gregory Boyle

Emotional health

- *Carry On, Warrior: The Power of Embracing Your Messy, Beautiful Life* by Glennon Doyle
- *The Dance of Anger: A Woman's Guide to Changing the Patterns of Intimate Relationships* by Harriet Lerner
- *Daring Greatly: How the Courage to Be Vulnerable Transforms the Way We Live, Love, Parent, and Lead* by Brené Brown
- *The Emotionally Healthy Church: A Strategy for Discipleship That Actually Changes Lives* by Peter Scazzero, Warren Bird, and Layton Ford
- *Emotionally Healthy Spirituality: Unleash a Revolution in Your Life in Christ* by Peter Scazzero
- *The Gift of Being Yourself: The Sacred Call to Self-Discovery* by David G. Benner
- *The Gifts of Imperfection: Let Go of Who You Think You're Supposed to Be and Embrace Who You Are* by Brené Brown
- *Healing through the Dark Emotions: The Wisdom of Grief, Fear, and Despair* by Miriam Greenspan
- *I Quit!: Stop Pretending Everything Is Fine and Change Your Life* by Geri Scazzero and Peter Scazzero
- *The Language of Letting Go: Daily Mediations for Codependents* by Melody Beattie
- *Rising Strong: The Reckoning, the Rumble, the Revolution* by Brené Brown
- *The Road Back to You: An Enneagram Journey to Self-Discovery* by Ian Morgan Cron and Suzanne Stabile
- *Seven Desires of Every Heart: Looking Past What Separates Us to Discover What Connects Us* by Mark Laaser and Debbie Laaser
- *Shattered Dreams: God's Unexpected Path to Joy* by Larry Crabb
- *The Soul of Shame: Retelling the Stories We Believe about Ourselves* by Curt Thompson

Spiritual practices, such as the disciplines of slowing, self-care, rest, waiting, blessing others, questioning, caring for the body, forgiving, *lectio divina*, grieving, or sabbath

- *An Altar in the World: A Geography of Faith* by Barbara Brown Taylor
- *The Body Keeps the Score: Brain, Mind, and Body in the Healing of Trauma* by Bessel van der Kolk
- *The Book of Forgiving: The Fourfold Path for Healing Ourselves and Our World* by Desmond Tutu and Mpho Tutu
- *Centering Prayer and Inner Awakening* by Cynthia Bourgeault
- *The Cure for Sorrow: A Book of Blessings for Times of Grief* by Jan Richardson
- *The Dance of the Dissident Daughter: A Woman's Journey from Christian Tradition to the Sacred Feminine* by Sue Monk Kidd
- *Embracing the Body: Finding God in Our Flesh and Bone* by Tara M. Owens
- *Everything Belongs: The Gift of Contemplative Prayer* by Richard Rohr
- *A Grace Disguised: How the Soul Grows through Loss* by Jerry Sittser
- *Inspired: Slaying Giants, Walking on Water, and Loving the Bible Again* by Rachel Held Evans
- *Into the Silent Land: A Guide to the Christian Practice of Contemplation* by Martin Laird
- *Liturgy of the Ordinary: Sacred Practices in Everyday Life* by Tish Harrison Warren
- *Practicing Our Faith: A Way of Life for a Searching People*, edited by Dorothy C. Bass
- *Sensible Shoes: A Story About the Spiritual Journey* by Sharon Garlough Brown
- *Soulful Spirituality: Becoming Fully Alive and Deeply Human* by David G. Benner
- *Spiritual Disciplines Handbook: Practices That Transform Us* by Adele Ahlberg Calhoun

- *To Bless the Space Between Us: A Book of Blessings* by John O'Donohue
- *Too Deep for Words: Rediscovering Lectio Divina* by Thelma Hall
- *Welcoming Prayer: Consent on the Go* by Pamela Begeman, Mary Dwyer, Cherry Haisten, Gail Fizpatrick-Hopler, and Therese Saulnier
- *When the Heart Waits: Spiritual Direction for Life's Sacred Questions* by Sue Monk Kidd

NOTES

Introduction

1. Barbara Brown Taylor, *Learning to Walk in the Dark* (San Francisco: HarperOne, 2014), 129.
2. C. S. Lewis, *The Voyage of the Dawn Treader* (New York: Collier Books, 1970), 160.

Chapter 1: Good Grief

1. Richard Rohr, "Transforming Pain," *Daily Mediations*, October 17, 2018, accessed September 28, 2020, https://cac.org/transforming-pain-2018-10-17/.
2. "When Grief Gets Physical," *What's Your Grief*, accessed October 19, 2019, https://whatsyourgrief.com/physical-grief-symptoms/.
3. Jerry Sittser, *A Grace Disguised: How the Sould Grows Through Loss* (Grand Rapids, MI: Zondervan, 2004), 99–100.
4. James Finley, "The Spirituality of Trauma and Healing," workshop held on February 12, 2015 at Carmelite Spiritual Center, Darien, IL.
5. Sue Monk Kidd, *When the Heart Waits: Spiritual Direction for Life's Sacred Questions* (San Francisco: HarperSanFrancisco, 1992), 135–36.
6. Sally Lloyd-Jones, *The Story of God's Love for You* (Grand Rapids, MI: Zondervan, 2015), 109.

Chapter 2: God as Midwife, Not Rescuer

1. *ABC World News Tonight with Diane Sawyer*, December 7, 2010, accessed September 29, 2020, https://archive.org/details/KGO_20101208_013000 _ABC_World_News_With_Diane_Sawyer/start/1620/end/1680/.
2. Kathleen Norris, *Amazing Grace: A Vocabulary of Faith* (New York: Riverhead Books, 1998), 62.
3. Michael Card, *A Sacred Sorrow: Reaching Out to God in the Lost Language of Lament* (Colorado Springs, CO: NavPress, 2005), 129.
4. Sue Monk Kidd, *When the Heart Waits: Spiritual Direction for Life's Sacred Questions* (San Francisco: HarperSanFrancisco, 1992), 28.

5. "Midwife," *Merriam-Webster.com*, accessed May 29, 2020, https://merriam -webster.com/dictionary/midwife.

6. Helen Cepero, *Journaling as a Spiritual Practice: Encountering God through Attentive Writing* (Downers Grove, IL: IVP Books, 2008), 106.

Chapter 3: Remain in My Love

1. David G. Benner, *Surrender to Love: Discovering the Heart of Christian Spirituality* (Downers Grove, IL: IVP Books, 2003), 17.

2. Sue Monk Kidd, *The Dance of the Dissident Daughter: A Woman's Journey from Christian Tradition to the Sacred Feminine* (San Francisco: Harper-SanFrancisco, 1996), 4.

3. Brené Brown, *The Gifts of Imperfection: Let Go of Who You Think You're Supposed to Be and Embrace Who You Are* (Center City, MN: Hazelden, 2010), 37.

4. Henri J. M. Nouwen, *Life of the Beloved: Spiritual Living in a Secular World* (New York: Crossroad, 1992), 36.

5. Anthony de Mello, SJ quoted in *Hearts on Fire: Praying with Jesuits*, ed. Michael Harter, SJ (Chicago: Loyola Press, 1993), 8.

6. Gregory Boyle, *Tattoos on the Heart: The Power of Boundless Compassion* (New York: Free Press, 2010), 71.

7. Henri J. M. Nouwen, *The Return of the Prodigal Son: A Story of Homecoming* (New York: Image, 1994), 43.

8. Nouwen, *The Return of the Prodigal Son*, 74.

9. Danielle Shroyer, *Original Blessing: Putting Sin in its Rightful Place* (Minneapolis: Fortress, 2016), 197.

10. Benner, *Surrender to Love*, 89.

Chapter 4: It's a Both/And

1. *The Collected Works of C. G. Jung*, vol. 12, ed. William McGuire et al. (Princeton, NJ: Princeton University Press, 1968), 15

2. "Paradox," *Online Etymology Dictionary*, accessed February 21, 2020, https://www.etymonline.com/word/paradox.

3. Richard Rohr, *Everything Belongs: The Gift of Contemplative Prayer*, rev. ed. (New York: Crossroad, 2003), 20-21.

4. *The Collected Works of C.G. Jung*, vol. 13, ed. William McGuire et al. (Princeton, NJ: Princeton University Press, 1983), 16.

Chapter 5: Olly Olly Oxen Free: Community

1. Fulghum, *All I Ever Really Needed to Know I Learned in Kindergarten*, 58.

2. May Sarton, "Now I Become Myself," *Collected Poems (1930-1993)* (New York: W. W. Norton, 1993), 162.

3. "Olly Olly Oxen Free," *Wikipedia*, accessed May 26, 2020, https:// en.wikipedia.org/wiki/Olly_olly_oxen_free.

4. Parker J. Palmer, *Let Your Life Speak: Listening for the Voice of Vocation* (San Francisco: Jossey-Bass, 2000), 7.

5. Rachel Naomi Remen, M.D., *Kitchen Table Wisdom: Stories that Heal* (New York: Riverhead Books, 1996), 220.

6. Brené Brown, *Braving the Wilderness: The Quest for True Belonging and the Courage to Stand Alone* (New York: Random House, 2017), 59.

7. Parker J. Palmer, "On Staying at the Table: A Spirituality of Community." The essay has circulated widely since its initial publication in 1986 in the newsletter of a now-defunct Benedictine retreat center. Parker Palmer provided a copy of the essay as a PDF for this book on September 1, 2020.

8. Palmer, "On Staying at the Table"

Chapter 6: Clean Anger

1. James Finley, "The Spirituality of Trauma and Healing," workshop held on February 12, 2015 at Carmelite Spiritual Center, Darien, IL.

2. Emma Byrne, *Swearing Is Good for You: The Amazing Science of Bad Language* (New York: W. W. Norton, 2018), 46–48.

3. Miranda Larbi, "Swearing Is Good for You, According to Science," *New York Post*, April 19, 2019, accessed Sept. 29, 2020, https://nypost .com/2019/04/19/swearing-is-good-for-you-according-to-science/.

4. Brené Brown, *Braving the Wilderness: The Quest for True Belonging and the Courage to Stand Alone* (New York: Random House, 2017), 25.

5. Glennon Doyle Melton, *Carry On, Warrior: The Power of Embracing Your Messy, Beautiful Life* (New York: Scribner, 2014), 205.

6. Melanie Weidner, "I Mean Thank You," *Listen for Joy*, accessed September 29, 2020, https://listenforjoy.com/products/i-mean-thank-you.

7. Jan Richardson, "Blessing in the Anger," *The Cure for Sorrow: A Book of Blessings for Times of Grief* (Orlando, FL: Wanton Gospeller Press, 2016), 50.

Chapter 7: Take Off That Ugly Sweater: A Look at Shame

1. Curt Thompson, *The Soul of Shame: Retelling the Stories We Believe about Ourselves* (Downers Grove, IL: IVP Books, 2015), 23.

2. Brené Brown, *The Gifts of Imperfection: Let Go of Who You Think You're Supposed to Be and Embrace Who You Are* (Center City, MN: Hazelden, 2010), 38

3. Curt Thompson, *The Soul of Shame*, 24–25.

4. Kelly Gerken, "I Beg You: Please, Don't Grief Shame Me," *Still Standing Magazine* (July 30, 2018), accessed May 29, 2020, https://stillstanding mag.com/2018/07/30/i-beg-you-please-dont-grief-shame-me/.

5. John Bradshaw, *Healing the Shame That Binds You* (Deerfield Beach, FL: Health Communications, 1988), 10.

6. Bart Sumner, "It's the Shame," *The Grief Toolbox*, accessed May 29, 2020, https://thegrieftoolbox.com/article/its-shame.

7. Brown, *The Gifts of Imperfection*, 40.

8. Kelly Gerken, "The Cloak of Shame," *Still Standing Magazine* (March 4, 2018), accessed May 29, 2020, https://stillstandingmag.com/2018/03/04/the-cloak-of-shame/.

9. Thomas Keating, *The Human Condition: Contemplation and Transformation* (New York: Paulist Press, 1999), 34.

Chapter 8: It's a Marathon, Not a Sprint: Forgiveness as a Process

1. Jerry Sittser, *A Grace Disguised: How the Soul Grows Through Loss* (Grand Rapids, MI: Zondervan, 2004), 105.

2. Sue Monk Kidd, *The Dance of the Dissident Daughter: A Woman's Journey from Christian Tradition to the Sacred Feminine* (San Francisco: Harper-SanFrancisco, 1996), 190.

3. Desmond A. Tutu and Mpho A. Tutu, *The Book of Forgiving* (San Francisco: HarperOne, 2014), 34.

4. Sittser, *A Grace Disguised*, 144.

5. "Liminal Spaces," *Cambridge Art Association*, accessed on March 15, 2020, http://www.cambridgeart.org/liminal-spaces/.

Chapter 9: Welcoming What Is

1. Richard Rohr, "Tune Our Hearts," *Daily Meditations*, March 10, 2017, accessed May 30, 2020, https://cac.org/tune-our-hearts-2017-03-10/.

2. Richard Rohr, "Trust and Surrender," *Daily Mediations*, March 7, 2017, accessed May 30, 2020, https://cac.org/trust-and-surrender-2017-03-07/.

3. David G. Benner, *Sacred Companions: The Gift of Spiritual Friendship and Direction* (Downers Grove, IL: InterVarsity Press, 2002), 53.

4. Quoted in *Welcoming Prayer: Consent on the Go* by Pamela Begeman, Mary Dwyer, Cherry Haisten, Gail Fitzpatrick-Hopler, and Therese Saulnier (Wilkes-Barre, PA: Contemplative Outreach, 2014), 10.

5. Brian Zahnd, *Sinners in the Hands of a Loving God: The Scandalous Truth of the Very Good News* (Colorado Springs, CO: Waterbrook, 2017), 67.

6. Mary Mrozowski, "The Welcoming Prayer," *Contemplative Outreach*, accessed November 16, 2020, https://www.contemplativeoutreach.org/wp-content/uploads/2012/09/welcoming_prayer_trifold_2016.pdf.

Chapter 10: Embracing Our Bodies

1. Jane Kenyon, "Cages," *Collected Poems* (Minneapolis: Graywolf Press, 2005), 40.
2. Gabor Mate, introduction to *In an Unspoken Voice: How the Body Releases Trauma and Restores Goodness* by Peter Levine (Berkeley: North Atlantic Books, 2010), viii.
3. Bessel van der Kolk, *The Body Keeps the Score: Brain, Mind, and Body in the Healing of Trauma* (New York: Penguin Books, 2014), 81.
4. Nadia Bolz-Weber, "Sex; A Benediction: A Blessing for Our Bodies," *The Corners* (blog), March 3, 2020, accessed March 15, 2020, https://nadia bolzweber.substack.com/p/sex-a-benediction.
5. Peter A. Levine, *Healing Trauma: A Pioneering Program for Restoring the Wisdom of Your Body* (Boulder, CO: Sounds True, 2005), 10.
6. Deb Laaser, Heather L. Putney, Matthew Bundick, David L. Delmonico, Elizabeth J. Griffin, "Posttraumatic Growth in Relationally Betrayed Women," *Journal of Marital and Family Therapy* (43:3, July 2017): 435–47.

Chapter 11: The Larger Story

1. Bent Mohn, "Talk with Isak Dinesen," *New York Times Book Review*, November 3, 1957, section T, 284.
2. Rachel Held Evans, *Inspired: Slaying Giants, Walking on Water, and Loving the Bible Again* (Nashville, TN: Nelson Books, 2018), 47.
3. Walter Bruggeman, *Sabbath as Resistance: Saying No to the Culture of Now* (Louisville, KY: Westminster John Knox, 2014), 2.
4. Rabbi Hayyim Angel, "From Black Fire to White Fire: Conversations About Religious Tanakh Methodology," *Ideals* (27, Winter 2017/5777): 1-9.
5. Judy Petersen, "696: Delivered," February 13, 2020, *Vox Veniae*, podcast, voxveniae.com/2020/02/delivered.

Appendix A: Depression and Trauma

1. American Psychiatric Association, *Diagnostic and Statistical Manual of Mental Disorders*, 5th ed. (Arlington, VA: American Psychiatric Publishing, 2013), 160-63.
2. *Diagnostic and Statistical Manual of Mental Disorders*, 271–73.